Series / Number 04-012

Civil Disobedience and Civil Deviance

TERENCE BALL
University of Minnesota

 **SAGE PUBLICATIONS** / Beverly Hills / London

For information address:

SAGE PUBLICATIONS, INC.
275 South Beverly Drive
Beverly Hills, California 90212

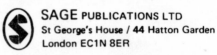

SAGE PUBLICATIONS LTD
St George's House / 44 Hatton Garden
London EC1N 8ER

International Standard Book Number 0-8039-0359-6

Library of Congress Catalog Card No. 73-92214

FIRST PRINTING

When citing a professional paper, please use the proper form. Remember to cite the
correct Sage Professional Paper series title and include the paper number. One of the
two following formats can be adapted (depending on the style manual used):

(1) NAGEL, S. S. (1973) "Comparing Elected and Appointed Judicial Systems."
Sage Professional Papers in American Politics, 1, 04-001. Beverly Hills, and London:
Sage Pubns.

OR

(2) Nagel, Stuart S. 1973. *Comparing Elected and Appointed Judicial Systems.* Sage
Professional Papers in American Politics, vol. 1, series no. 04-001. Beverly Hills and
London: Sage Publications.

CONTENTS

Civil Disobedience and Civil Deviance

TERENCE BALL
University of Minnesota

I. INTRODUCTION

Civil disobedience, while now largely passé in practice, continues never-theless to pose some interesting and important theoretical questions about obligation and authority in a democracy. Although such questions are, I suspect, without final answer, they are at least open to clarification. Clarification may take either (or both) of two forms: conceptual and historical. In the first, one is concerned to explicate the meaning of concepts such as authority, freedom, obligation, and so on. In the second, one looks for the sources of these ideas, and traces their development through time. In this essay I shall take the latter approach. For it seems to be that the relative quiet—perhaps even quiescence—of politics in the early 1970s affords us a unique opportunity for reflecting upon the turbulence of the preceding decade, and more particularly upon the "theoretical" import of civil disobedience and its ethical justification.

With an irony that was surely not intended, the National Commission on the Causes and Prevention of Violence (1969) submitted its final report to the nation in the closing hours of the troubled decade of the 1960s. Yet the irony involved more than a matter of timing. For the same commission which had made bold inquiries into violence found itself unalterably

AUTHOR'S NOTE: *For their criticism and encouragement in the writing of this essay, I thank John Schaar, Norman Jacobson, Mason Drukman, George Von der Muhll, John Ruggie and Peter Euben.*

divided over nonviolence. The divisive issue was whether civil disobedience is ever justified. Unable to compromise and so speak with one voice, as before, the Commission on this occasion spoke with two voices, one in an official recommendation, the other in a dissenting minority report.

The majority agreed that democracy is always ill-served by acts of civil disobedience. In its view, to publicly disobey the law, for whatever reason, is to sow the wind and to risk reaping the whirlwind of anarchy. Unfortunately, the opportunity for a genuinely public exchange about the nature and limits of political obligation was forfeited when the majority resurrected the tired spectre of anarchy. Nothing could have more effectively terminated the conversation. In figuratively hoisting the black flag of anarchy—not as a standard but as a warning—the majority assumed what it was obliged to prove, namely that civilly disobedient acts tend to be self-multiplying and potentially limitless in size and effect.

The dissenting minority hastened to note that, on the contrary, the supposed "anarchic" tendencies of civil disobedience have never materialized. It may well be, they contended, that civil disobedience may preclude violence and anarchy by serving public notice that minorities are being mistreated or neglected, thereby paving the way for their recognition, accommodation and integration into the political system. In the long run, civil disobedience may actually strengthen and stabilize a liberal democratic polity.

Yet, divided as they were, both factions were allied in principle; they appeared to disagree only about several matters of fact. In principle, both sides agreed that social order and stability is a positive good and that, while dissent should be protected in a free society, its protection should not extend beyond limits that might endanger social order. They disagreed, in the main, about whether civil disobedience meets these criteria of justification. Their two lines of argument are hardly new, and I do not propose to examine the relative validity or merit of either. My starting point in this essay is not their disagreement but rather their remarkable similarity. For both sides share the unquestioned premise that the standard for judging political action is to be found not in the intentions of the actors, nor in the justice of their cause, but in the social effects of their action. Social consequences are taken to count for more than moral intentions and arguments, and men's actions are to be judged according to whether they contribute to or detract from social stability. This standard is characteristic of liberal utilitarianism. It is also characteristically American.

In this essay I propose to identify several modes of justifying disobedience. The first and historically dominant mode is that of liberalism, which has two more or less distinguishable strands: an older one deriving from natural law, and associated preeminently with Locke and later with Jefferson; and a more recent one deriving from utilitarianism, and associated with Madison, Paley, and many latter-day liberals. I shall roughly sketch the contours of their respective rationales for political resistance. This is followed by a more detailed examination of a second, subdominant mode of justifying disobedience: that of Thoreauvian radicalism. The final portion of the essay examines a still newer mode of justifying disobedience: the sociology of deviant behavior, which views civil disobedience as a type of potentially "functional" social "deviance." I shall try to disinter the liberal-utilitarian assumptions of this functionalist approach to the justification of civil disobedience—or, to coin a neologism, "civil deviance"—and to criticize some of its implications.

Needless to say, what follows is in no sense definitive, nor is it meant to be. My aims in this essay are frankly exploratory and suggestive. To that end, I have excluded much that properly belongs to a discussion of civil disobedience—for example, religious and legal considerations. My reasons for not treating these historically important matters will, I hope, become apparent as the essay proceeds.

II. LIBERALISM, UTILITARIANISM, AND RESISTANCE

Any inquiry into the foundations of American liberalism must take account of the political thought of John Locke, whose influence has been pervasive and profound (Curti, 1937; Hartz, 1955; Bailyn, 1967; Dunn, 1969a). Locke, says Louis Hartz (1955: 140), is a "massive national cliché." He was regarded by colonial Americans, Rossiter (1963: 70) tells us, as "a famous, almost unassailable English philosopher who had glorified a rebellion *(sic)* of Englishmen against an English king," and was indeed "the most popular source of Revolutionary ideas."[1] Had he not proclaimed a "right" of revolution? On the face of it, Lockean doctrine appears to be "radical," even to our modern eyes. Yet, when we examine the conditions under which this right of revolution applies, when we analyze its underlying *raison,* we can see that its implications are far from radical.

Locke draws a distinction between rebellion and revolution. Whereas revolution can be justified, rebellion cannot. For Locke, contract rather than individual conscience is the basis of civil society; and, by implication, the violation of contract justifies disobedience on the part of the injured party. Anyone, whether king or commoner, who violates the social contract puts himself into a "state of war" with his fellows (Locke, 1960: 464-465). Having entered into such a state of war, he is considered to be in rebellion against society, and his proper punishment is death (Locke, 1960: 464, 467). However, rebellion and revolution are by no means identical; the two terms are not interchangeable. For revolution is the contractually sanctioned *collective, social* attempt to reestablish the social contract and set it aright after legally constituted authorities have taken illegal or extra-contractual steps—for example, when the "legislature is altered," or when either the legislature or the prince "act contrary to their trust" (Locke, 1960: 455, 460).[2]

Revolution, unlike rebellion, is the act of an offended majority. As for the individual, he has recourse to resistance only as a member of a collectivity, not as a private person. Not individual conscience, but the aggregation of private interests, provides the basis for justifying revolution. The "right" of revolution is a corollary of the liberal doctrine of property rights, which in turn are "natural" or God-given rights. The pursuit and protection of private interests constitute men's natural inclinations, including that of establishing civil society: "The reason why men enter into society is the preservation of their property" (Locke, 1960: 460). The impetus for establishing government is individualistic, but the consequence is collectivistic. Conscience or "private judgment" could be exercised only outside of civil society, in the state of nature; but this prerogative is surrendered when the individual contracts with his fellows and enters civil society. In Locke's hands, as Sheldon Wolin (1960: 338) notes, "conscience surrendered what had been its most striking aspect, its individual quality; it became, instead, a social or collective form of judgment." This was "a new kind of conscience, social rather than individual, . . . an internalized expression of external rules rather than the externalized expression of internal convictions." Conscience, in other words, had been effectively socialized; it became "other-directed."

If liberalism had effectively collectivized conscience, it followed that the common social standards or norms could not be at odds with individual conscience, since the latter was the former writ small. The essential rightness of the common standard had been enshrined in the axioms of natural law, which all "reasonable" men could know. The effect was of course to sanctify conformity. As Hartz (1955: 11) remarks, Lockean liberalism "had a conformitarian germ to start with, since natural law told equal men equal things." It is this liberal penchant for conformity which intrigued and frightened Tocqueville, and has engaged the attention of modern social scientists and historians such as David Riesman and Louis Hartz. We shall have occasion to return to natural law and its conformitarian implications when we consider Thoreau's criticisms of American liberalism.

Whereas Locke had regarded the preservation of "life, liberty and property" as the proper end of government, Jefferson proclaimed "life, liberty, and the pursuit of happiness" as the end of civil society. This is true not only of the ringing passages of the Declaration of Independence, but is repeatedly expressed in his private correspondence as well (Jefferson, 1955: 58). While using many of the terms and concepts of Lockean liberalism, Jefferson nevertheless appeared to infuse them with new meaning. As Parrington (1927: 344) suggests, Jefferson's "substitution of 'pursuit of happiness' for 'property' marks a complete break with the Whiggish doctrine of property rights that Locke had bequeathed to the English middle class," and this substitution was made on purely idealistic grounds." To proclaim the pursuit of happiness as a "right" appears to be remarkably radical. But how radical was it? An answer to that question can perhaps be found in Jefferson's conception of happiness.

For Jefferson (1892, VI: 291), happiness is to be found outside politics, "in the lap and love of my family, in the society of my neighbors and my books, in the wholesome occupation of my farm and my affairs." Happiness is to be found in private activity, not political action. Politics is a necessary evil, an instrument or a means of protecting men in their private pursuits. Government does not so much promote public happiness as it prevents private unhappiness. Political action thus emerges, on this view, as a form of prevention.[3]

In Jefferson's view, the private enclave *par excellence* was the farm. His much-acclaimed trust in the "common man" was rather a faith in the farmer.[4] For the farmer is the model of the happy man; and men who are happy, in the privative liberal sense, will mind their own business. The common man should quite literally be free to cultivate his own garden. Jefferson's praise of privacy had a political counterpart. For when men are free to pursue their private interests they can be trusted. Private pursuits do not make men rapacious and greedy but, on the contrary, contain and limit their vision, turning it inward rather than outward, rendering it private rather than public. Men of such restricted vision are scarcely disposed to favor political action, except insofar as it may further their "happiness," which is to say their privacy.

Given such a conception of happiness, and the social arrangements which protect it, political conflict becomes largely superfluous. The conditions under which the right of revolution applies are simply not present. And because revolution is unnecessary, one may speak of it in an offhanded, almost casual way—as Jefferson in fact did. It was, however, quite a different matter when the spectre of a second American revolution seemed ready to materialize, for then President Jefferson was among the first to take alarm, preparing to exorcise the spectre with "a few wholesome prosecutions" (Levy, 1963).

For all his ringing remarks about the natural right of revolution, and the "right" of every generation to abolish the government of their fathers, Jefferson's outlook was subtended by a strong utilitarian strain which became more marked in his later years. Natural rights, including the right of revolution, came to be subordinated to utilitarian considerations of convenience and expediency, until his position paralleled that of Locke and Madison. Locke, too, had spoken grandly of the right of revolution, although he qualified it by arguing that it may be more convenient to forbear and to tolerate injustice: "For till the mischief be grown general, and the ill-designs of the rulers become visible, or their attempts [evident] to the greater part, the people who are more disposed to suffer than right themselves by resistance are not apt to stir. The examples of particular injustice, or oppression of here and there an unfortunate man, move them not" (Locke, 1960: 466). In short, revolution is—except in very extreme circumstances shared by almost everyone—not only more trouble than it is worth, but is morally repugnant as well.

These essentially utilitarian attitudes are expressed in the language of natural law: if conditions are "really" unbearable, then all "reasonable" men will know as much, for the law of nature is equally accessible to all. The conformitarian corollary remains implicit: an individual or a minority must be defective in their reason, i.e., unreasonable, if they persist in criticizing conditions that the majority does not perceive as threatening. Moreover, if such criticism is translated into action, then the dissenting individual or minority has, in Lockean terms, entered into rebellion against civil society, and is deserving of death at its hands. Hence civil disobedience, as Thoreau was later to conceive of it, remained, within the dominant liberal framework, an inconceivable and unthinkable option, due to its very "unreasonableness" if not its sheer perversity.

It remained for Jefferson's younger friend Madison to make explicit the utilitarian drift of this essentially Lockean argument. Madison argued that one of the defining characteristics of democracy—the principle of majority rule—was inconsistent with natural law, since a true law of nature would perforce entail not merely a majority consensus, but full unanimity of agreement among all reasonable men. Yet such unanimity was in practice impossible to attain. In reality, he argued, the authority of government and the obligation of citizens derives not from natural right but from a "compact founded on utility." Men obey the government because it is usually more convenient to obey than to resist. Individual consent rests upon expediency; one does not consent to government's authority so much as one tacitly *assents* to it (Madison, 1904: 438-439). Jefferson (1892, XV: 470-471) also came to speak of "tacit assent" as the grounds of political obligation. In this way he undercut his own endorsement of each generation's right to alter or abolish the government of its fathers. The right of revolution became, in the end, little more than a rhetorical device to be used by orators on the Fourth of July. Surrounded by a *cordon sanitaire* of utilitarian qualifications, the right of revolution was made safe for democracy.

While Jefferson and Madison were corresponding privately, similar conclusions were being publicly propounded by William Paley, an English clergyman. Paley had published his *Principles of Moral and Political Philosophy* in 1785, and by the time of Jefferson's death in 1826, it had become a standard text for Americans interested in moral and political questions. Paley's book was a rather bizarre amalgam of Anglican theology and utilitarianism, expressed in the language of Lockean natural law and natural rights. As Wilson Smith (1954: 415) remarks, Paley "seiz[ed] Locke's creation—this moral child with no innate morality, possessed of a desire for happiness and the right to life, liberty, and property—[and] spirited him away to his own philosophical nursery. Here he put him in theological undergarments, taught him that 'whatever is expedient is right', and then clothed him for the world of affairs with a suit of Lockean natural rights."[5] Except for their theological accoutrements, Paley's conclusions exhibited at least a family resemblance to those of Madison and Jefferson, who had in their own way attempted to combine natural law and utilitarianism.[6]

Paley's (1785) attempt to combine utilitarianism with traditional natural law is ingenious if not altogether persuasive. He argued, first, that men are not creatures of reason but of habit and prejudice. Men are moved to action by their own private interests. This human tendency is habitual and therefore "natural." The norms or standards of human conduct are empirical in character; that is, men do in fact act as they should, even if pious moralists deem their actions selfish. Men tend to act in ways that are most expedient in realizing their own private ends. Moral conduct thus becomes a matter of expediency and calculations of advantage. Lest this sound un-Christian, Paley made another claim: the principle of utility is the law of God. That is, whatever most men do is "natural"; God is the author of all that is natural; men tend to act on the basis of habit, convenience, expediency and advantage; therefore convenience or expediency is the proper ground for human morality. Even if men's motives are selfish or base, the wider social consequences will, in the end, be beneficial. Selfishly motivated action leads to incremental adjustments in society as a whole, thereby making it more stable and peaceful in the long run.

Paley's model for moral and political conduct is the self-regulating and self-adjusting market of liberal political economy. Paley's ethic of beneficient selfishness is the moral counterpart of Adam Smith's "invisible hand," or of Bernard Mandeville's *Fable of the Bees:* "Thus every part was full of vice/ Yet the whole mass a Paradise/ . . . Such were the blessings of that State/ Their crimes conspired to make them great." For Paley, the invisible hand is the hand of God. Greed, vice and selfishness are all part of His plan.

Such a model of human action most emphatically does not, however, license just any sort of behavior, but only that which will prove to be most convenient and most advantageous to every egoistic individual. Expediency can be a hard taskmaster. A mistaken calculation of advantage, a wrong weighing of costs incurred and benefits gained, can result in misery and unhappiness, both for oneself and for others.

When Paley applied his "economistic" model of morality to political action, resistance to government came to rest upon the same grounds as political obligation and moral conduct generally, namely expediency or convenience. One may "naturally" or rightfully resist the dictates of government whenever the costs of obedience outweigh the disadvantages of resistance. One's actions ought to follow the path of least resistance, or rather, the low road of greater personal convenience. As it happens, resistance is rarely worth the effort or inconvenience it requires. An individual or a minority cannot be effective; without majority approval and support, their efforts at resistance are necessarily wasteful and inconvenient, not merely for the dissenting minority, but for the public at large (the latter being "inconvenienced" in having to suppress the former). In other words, if one finds oneself outnumbered, the path of least resistance is to do nothing at all. Minority or individual disobedience would, on this reckoning, be a waste of time and energy.

In one crucial respect, Paley's conclusions paralleled Locke's. Individual resistance or disobedience is inconceivable and inadmissable. Resistance is the prerogative of inconvenienced majorities; it is not a right belonging to morally wronged minorities. What first appears to be a vindication of a radical or even anarchic individualism turns out, in the end, to be a rationalization for the most stringent and cloying sort of conformism.[7]

At least one of Paley's American readers was highly critical of his conformitarian and complacent outlook. He was Henry David Thoreau of Massachusetts.

III. THOREAU: THE MORAL BASIS OF
INDIVIDUAL RESISTANCE

In an undemocratic state resistance is primarily a practical problem. In a democratic state, however, resistance is primarily a moral problem. How can one justifiably take it upon oneself to alter or abolish those practices and arrangements which have supposedly been sanctioned, either expressly or tacitly, by the will of the majority? It has frequently been claimed that disobedience in a democracy is practically unnecessary and morally perverse. Because of the institutional arrangements of liberal democracy, it is said, one cannot without contradiction be both disobedient and democratic. Is there no way to reconcile the two? Surely such a reconciliation would involve nothing less than a critique of liberal democracy, and perhaps an alternative conception of democracy itself. This is, in some measure, precisely what Thoreau attempted to provide.

In the partial reconstruction of Thoreau's argument which follows, I shall try to indicate several things. First, contrary to a popular interpretation, Thoreau was hostile to natural law and natural right. Secondly, he rejected utilitarianism, but only in part. Thirdly, he was no "anarchist," as some have claimed, but rather offered an alternative vision of democracy, especially as regards the principle of majority rule. If Thoreau was in fact an anarchist, then perhaps those who share a commitment to democracy need not take him very seriously. I shall argue, however, that Thoreau was a democrat, albeit an unconventional one, and that he had some important things to say about democratic theory. Unfortunately, a reconstruction of Thoreau's justificatory argument—and a rebuttal to some of the more serious charges of his critics—will occasionally require some rather close textual analysis. This procedure is necessitated by the very structure of Thoreau's argument, which is a stylistic tour de force, employing hyperbole, irony, double entendre, puns, and other devices to make his most important points. His literary virtuosity has been a source of much confusion to his less sensitive readers, whose flat-footed literalism has led them to mistake Thoreau's meaning.[8]

The dominant liberal tradition of American political thought deals with obligation and disobedience by a peculiar form of argument. It proceeds from the whole to the parts, and from first premises to final, prescriptive conclusions. This form of argument relies upon certain assumptions—natural law and natural rights, the stated ends of government, the primacy of privacy, social utility, and so on—and from these are derived ethical maxims and standards of judgment. Yet with Thoreau a different style of argument emerges. He wishes to argue the other way around, starting with a given situation and working out some justifiable course of action from that point. More than argumentative style, however, separates Thoreau from the liberal tradition of American political thought. The whole substance of Thoreau's position differs radically from the Lockean tradition. And this radical difference is nowhere more evident than in his rejection of natural law as the grounds of obligation and justifiable disobedience.

Whenever Thoreau speaks of natural law or "higher law," it is always in a mordant, ironic way. "They only can force me who obey a higher law than I," he says in *Civil Disobedience* (Thoreau, 1893c: 376). To take such a statement as a literal endorsement of the natural law thesis (Drinnon, 1962; Eulau, 1962) is to mistake his meaning, and to become mired in inconsistency and contradiction. For this would posit a law that is "higher" than individual conscience, which Thoreau takes for his guide. Moreover, since natural law purports to be equally accessible to all men of reason, Thoreau would have to count himself either unreasonable or perverse, since otherwise he should not have to be "forced" to obey what is transparently evident to others. In *A Plea for Captain John Brown* Thoreau (1893: 438) argues for the ethical primacy of individual conscience, claiming that individuals and not lawyers should argue "cases of the highest importance." "Let lawyers decide trivial cases," he says, immediately "qualifying" this statement by remarking in an almost off-handed way, "*If* they were the interpreters of the everlasting laws which rightfully bind man, *that* would be another thing." It soon becomes apparent, however, that this qualification is gratuitous, for he asks, "What kind of laws for free men can you expect from that?" A free man is bound only by his conscience in moral matters. There is no court of appeal, no "law" higher than one's own conscience.

Thoreau's critique of the Lockean-liberal nexus between natural law and political obligation takes several forms. One of these is his penchant for punning on legal and political words like "constitution." In *Slavery in Massachusetts,* he says

> The judges and lawyers, . . . and all men of expediency, try this case [of an escaped slave named Anthony Burns, whose owner had petitioned the state of Massachusetts for the return of his 'property'] by a very low and incompetent standard. They consider, not whether the Fugitive Slave Law is right, but whether it is what they call *constitutional.* Is virtue constitutional, or vice? Is equity constitutional, or iniquity? (Thoreau, 1893c: 401)

Then he mounts a mordant attack on the Lockean version of the natural law thesis, concentrating on the absurdity of the social contract myth, with its corollary doctrine of "tacit consent" (a version of which is found also in Madison and Jefferson):

> The question is, not whether you or your grandfather seventy years ago, did not enter into agreement to serve the devil, and that service is not accordingly now due; but whether you will not now, for once and at last, serve God—in spite of your past recreancy, or that of your ancestor,—by obeying that eternal and only just CONSTI-TUTION, which He, and not any Jefferson or Adams, has written into your being (Thoreau, 1893c: 402).

On the face of it, this is a straightforward, even hackneyed, restatement of the natural law thesis. That it is so expressed is enough to make us suspicious of any literal interpretation. On closer examination, Thoreau's statement emerges as another pun on the word "constitution," playing upon its connotations of contract and consent while implying that consent is ultimately a matter of another sort of constitution, namely one's temperament and will. Thus he remarks, for example, that one's following, or failure to follow, one's conscience is "a matter of constitution and temperament, after all"; that "It is the difference of constitution, of intelligence and faith, and not streams and mountains, that make the true and impassable boundaries between individuals and between states"; and that the "Modern Democrat is not willfully but constitutionally blind" (Thoreau, 1893c: 445, 421, 444).[9]

In his political essays especially, Thoreau's outward playfulness masks a serious intent. This is most evident when he examines a key legal or political term, turning it, so to speak, so that the concept catches the light from different angles and refracts it to give various effects. In this way Thoreau tries to break the spell that our ordinary vocabulary casts over our way of seeing the political world. The language of natural law had circumscribed the range of possibilities for individuals, limiting their field of vision. Thoreau's satirizing of natural law, along with his playful examination of its key concepts, represented an attempt to let men look at their society and themselves in a new way. In this sense he has something in common with the Western tradition of political theory.[10]

If natural law and natural right offered no adequate grounds for justifying individual or minority disobedience, neither did utilitarianism. Thoreau had read Paley's *Principles of Moral and Political Philosophy,* and had taken strong exception to its early formulation of utilitarian principles.

> Paley, a common authority with many on moral questions,... resolves all civil obligation into expediency; and he [Paley, 1785:

424] proceeds to say 'that so long as the interest of the whole society requires it, that is, so long as the established government cannot be resisted or changed without public inconvenience, it is the will of God that the established government be obeyed, and no longer. . . . This principle being admitted, the justice of every particular case of resistance is reduced to a computation of the quantity of the danger and grievance on the one side and of the probability and expense of redressing it on the other' (Thoreau, 1893c: 361)

The very idea of justice is thus emasculated through redefinition. Thoreau wishes to reinstate the ineffable moral dimension, the dimension of selfless free choice, in the concept of justice. Just action is hardly ever a matter of expediency and calculations of personal advantage. Nor can individual conscience be excluded from any calculation which purports to give answers to moral questions. Paley, he says,

appears never to have contemplated those cases to which the rule of expediency does not apply, in which a people, as well as an individual, must do justice, *cost what it may*. If I have unjustly wrested a plank from a drowning man, I must restore it to him though I drown myself. This, according to Paley, would be inconvenient. But he that would save his life, in such a case, shall lose it (Thoreau, 1893c: 362).

In short, justice may be costly and painful, but it is not for that reason to be abandoned in favor of injustice—or, more precisely, an emasculated redefinition of justice.

Thoreau's main concern, however, was not with metaethical considerations but with concrete injustices. The injustice of slavery, the Fugitive Slave Law, the Mexican War—all were uppermost in Thoreau's mind as he wrote his political essays. He was especially distressed that Americans who professed to abhor slavery could nevertheless oppose radical abolitionism, favoring instead a program of gradual reform. In support of this position, liberal gradualists often cited Paley; as Smith (1954: 421) remarks, "Paley's text well represented the gradualist position of many moralists in the early slavery debates." They argued that one must, in true utilitarian fashion, weigh the cost of abolishing slavery against the benefits to be gained for the society as a whole; and in this computation the program of the Abolitionists was found wanting. On the utilitarian ledger, the radical Abolitionists' demand for an end to slavery, no matter what the cost, was placed on the debit side, and hence was "unrealistic." Thoreau's response was vehement. The question of costs versus benefits ought not to enter into moral debates. Yet this is the way the question would invariably be posed for public decision. Even if the majority of Americans did vote to abolish slavery, "it will be because they are indifferent to slavery, or because there is little slavery to be abolished by their vote" (Thoreau, 1893c: 364-365). Some matters, he avers, are too important to be decided by taking a vote.[11]

The principle of majority rule is little more than a method or means of calculating preferences and interests; it is the political counterpart of the principle of utility, or, as Thoreau mockingly called it, "the rule of expediency." Thoreau's objection to the easy expedient of resorting to majority rule on *all* questions was of the same sort as his objection to Paley's utilitarianism. The "rule of expediency" is not universally applicable; more specifically, it should not be applied to moral decisions. Only individual conscience can properly decide moral issues.

More often than not, decisions left to the majority will be based on calculations of expediency and advantage. Electoral bodies, like all collectivities, are amoral (Thoreau, 1893c: 362-363).[12] The act of voting is anonymous; anonymity frees the voter from any concern with larger moral and political issues, reducing him to a selfish calculator of his own advantage. Voting is a method for anonymously and amorally registering one's own interests, regardless of whether one's preferences are noble or base. The act of voting thus emerges not as a public or a political act, but as a preeminently private and selfish affair.

> All voting is a sort of gaming, like checkers or backgammon, with a slight moral tinge to it, a playing with right or wrong, with moral questions. ... The character of the voter is not staked. [The obligation of the majority] never exceeds that of expediency. Even voting *for the right* is *doing* nothing for it. It is only expressing to men feebly your desire that it should prevail. A wise man will not leave the right to the mercy of chance (Thoreau, 1893c: 363).

Thoreau's reservations about the moral efficacy of majority rule have been taken, by some critics, as an indication of his hostility to democracy. As one critic (Mayo, 1960: 181-182) has recently charged, "... the fanatical Thoreau [believed] that a majority has no right *whatever* to rule a minority against its consent." Another asserts that Thoreau was "thoroughly muddled and confused because [he] implies both that one can accept democracy as a political system and also believe that every citizen has a right to overthrow it if *any* law passed by a democracy violates his obligation to the right" (Hook, 1964: 118). A closer reading of Thoreau will, however, show these charges to be misstated if not unfounded.[13]

Thoreau was a democrat who faced squarely and without hesitation the key issue of political obligation in a democracy: the paradox of conflicting commitments. On the one hand, a democrat is committed to the principle of majority rule; on the other, he cannot easily abandon his innermost convictions if he finds himself in the minority. He may even find himself in the rather paradoxical position of holding that two conflicting claims ought to be supported (Wollheim, 1962). When can one justifiably resist the will of the majority, and when is one obligated to obey it? Are all majority decisions equally obligatory? To what extent are the decisions of the majority morally binding on the minority? Can one be both disobedient and democratic? These are the sorts of vexing questions to which Thoreau implicitly addressed himself in his political essays, and especially in *Civil Disobedience*. In attempting to answer these questions, Thoreau made several important (yet still largely unrecognized) contributions to democratic theory, the most notable being his attempted solution to the paradox of conflicting commitments.

Contrary to the charges of his liberal critics, Thoreau does not resolve the paradox of conflicting commitments by asserting that the conscientious individual is never bound by the decision of the majority. Thoreau's solution is, rather to redefine the role of the majority, giving its utilitarian inclinations a free rein in non-moral matters. The decisions of the majority should bind all alike in matters which are ordinarily outside the moral realm. This results in a somewhat different image of democracy. "Can there not be," Thoreau (1893c: 358) asks, "a government in which majorities do not virtually decide right and wrong, but conscience?—in which majorities decide only those questions to which the rule of expediency is applicable?" He has no qualms about supporting government schemes for highways and schools, since these are not primarily moral matters; here the "rule of expediency" does apply, and is indeed an efficacious means of aggregating preferences.[14] In such circumstances the minority is obligated to go along with the decision of the majority. So long as the state refrains from meddling in moral matters, leaving such questions to individual conscience, Thoreau will submit.

But what kind of state is this? Thoreau's model state is at first sight a poor one, a non-moral skeleton of a policy which commands loyalty only because it does not transgress the prerogative of individual conscience. The fact is, Thoreau regards this vision of the democratic state as second-best, and a far cry from an ideal, "truly just" polity. He objects to the liberal state *not* because it makes demands upon him, but because it does not make the right kind of demands. It does not expect enough of him. It does not give him what the Greeks called a *bios politikos,* a second life, in which he may exercise his talents publicly and selflessly, and thereby attain distinction and nobility. Indeed, the liberal state recognizes no separation of public and private; it sees in the public realm only an extension of the private sphere in which self-interest predominates. In this state, as "in our daily intercourse with men, our nobler faculties are dormant and suffered to rust. None will pay us the compliment to expect nobleness from us. Though we have gold to give, they demand only copper" (Thoreau, , 1893a: 284). The only gold that a man can contribute to the state is in coin. The state expects little more than hard currency from its subjects. The only gold standard it knows is the literal one.

In spite of this, Thoreau will pay his highway and school taxes because, he says, "I am as desirous of being a good neighbor as I am of being a bad subject" (Thoreau, 1893c: 380). Yet the role of neighbor is hardly the noblest part a man may play; it may be preferable to being a subject, but it is not of a piece with citizenship. A man's best qualities are not revealed when he acts and speaks as a neighbor or even as a friend. His noblest characteristics are drawn out and developed only when he acts as a citizen.

Thoreau excoriates his state, on one occasion, not for tolerating individual abolitionists, but for failing to join them. Admirable as the Underground Railway was, it remained the responsibility of individuals acting de jure against the state. The state of Massachusetts is not doing *enough* in ignoring the presence of the illegal Railway; it should not merely tolerate, but be an active partisan of, such a just cause. Because individuals have had to assume the proper functions of the state, the state's authority is eroded until, at last, it seeks refuge in unimportant administrative tasks. "If private men are obligated to perform the offices of government, to protect the weak and dispense justice, then the government becomes only a hired man, or clerk, to perform menial or indifferent services." Yet any government which "recognizes and accepts this relation," he says, is "crazy." For the consequence will be that "the government, its salary being insured, withdraws into the back shop, taking the Constitution with it, and bestows most of its labor on repairing that" (Thoreau, 1893c: 431). When government becomes narrow and legalistic, rather than expansive and generous, it can no longer claim to represent its citizens (not "subjects"). "We talk about a *representative* government; but what a monster of a government is that where the noblest faculties of the mind, and the *whole* heart are *not* represented" (Thoreau, 1893c: 429). These are hardly the sentiments of an anarchist—or of a liberal either, for that matter.

In a similar vein, Thoreau criticized Mirabeau for having proclaimed, "I reason without obeying, when obedience appears to me contrary to reason"—and who had, to prove his point, become a part-time highway robber to test the mettle of his opposition to society. "A saner man," Thoreau remarked, "would have found opportunities enough to put himself in formal *[i.e., public]* opposition to the most sacred laws of society, and so test his resolution ... without violating ... his own nature." If a man's opposition is genuine, he will not be clandestine in his action, but public and open. He will not oppose for the sake of opposition, or to prove anything to himself; above all his stance "will *never* be one of opposition to a *just* government." Mirabeau and the anarchists are blind to any distinction between just and unjust government; in their view, no action taken by any government, real or imagined, is deserving of recognition, much less respect. Not so for Thoreau. He envisions the possibility, in the last sentence of *Civil Disobedience,* of "a still more perfect and glorious State, which ... I have imagined, but not yet anywhere seen." Yet the absence of such a state hardly justifies the "rabid virtue" of a Mirabeau or the pervasive opposition of an anarchist. "Cut the leather only where the shoe pinches. Let us not have a rabid virtue that will be revenged on society,—that falls on it, not like the morning dew, but like the fervid noonday sun, to wither it" (Thoreau, 1893a: 332-333; 1893b: 355).

Just as opposition should not be rabid and reflexive, so should obligation not be passive and unreflective. Thoreau's attitude toward the liberal state will usually be one of tolerance, but not of loyalty. He may excuse the state, but he will not defend it. Still, he adds, "Show me a free state, and a court truly of justice, and I will fight for them" (Thoreau, 1893c: 404). A good government enhances and enriches life, but a poor, timid, amoral state is of less value than a non-political association of "neighbors." A "good" government is one which makes full use of its potential for doing good. "The effect of a good government is to make life more valuable; of a bad one, to make it less valuable ..." (Thoreau, 1893c: 405). That is why he is quick to disassociate himself from the anarchists of his time. "Unlike those who call themselves no-government men, I ask for, not at once no government, but at once a better government." He makes this plea not as a subject, but, as he explicitly remarks, as a *citizen.* [15] It is better to be a good neighbor than a good subject; but better by far to be a good citizen in a just state.

It now becomes clearer why Thoreau's liberal critics have regarded him as an anarchist. [16] For he sometimes *did* seem to favor the abolition of the state—the liberal state, in which democracy and the principle of majority rule were methods of registering and implementing private (usually economic) interests, with government acting only as a benign and bloodless "broker." The liberal state provides virtually no "public space" in which an individual may rise to his full stature; instead, by treating all preferences—whether just or unjust, selfless or selfish—as "interests" to be tallied, it exercises a limiting and levelling effect, reducing citizenship to its lowest common denominator and political action to a matter of calculating one's own advantage in a market situation. Thoreau's objections to the market model of democracy are penned in acid. Noting that his fellow townspeople had dismissed John Brown's radical abolitionist activities as irrational because he did not "gain anything" in undertaking them, Thoreau retorted, "Well, no, I don't suppose he could get four-and-sixpence a day for being hung, take the year around." But expediency is not tantamount to citizenship; a good citizen will not be content with weighing personal costs against public benefits, gains against losses, convenience against inconvenience. Apply the language of economics to bartering and trading, not to public action. "No doubt you can get more in your market for a quart of milk than for a quart of blood, but that is not the market that heroes carry their blood to" (Thoreau, 1893c: 418). In a similar vein, Thoreau (1893c: 380-381) emphasized that his refusal to pay his poll tax was not a question of money but of morality, not of principal but of principle.

Doing right is rarely convenient or expedient; more often it is inconvenient, difficult, even dangerous. Paley's market model of morality, like the market model of liberal democracy, reduces action to convenience. To act rationally and rightly is, on this view, to follow the path of least resistance. Thoreau defines expediency as "choosing that course which offers the slightest obstacles to the feet, that is, a down-hill one." But, he adds, "there is no such thing as accomplishing a righteous reform by the use of 'expediency.' There is no such thing as sliding up-hill. In morals the only sliders are backsliders" (Thoreau, 1893c: 402). A society in which every subject slides downhill may be stable yet morally impoverished.

Civil disobedience is not undertaken, nor retrospectively justified, on grounds of expediency. It is not one way of sliding among others, but a kind of "friction" (Thoreau, 1893c: 368). By going against the common grain, it calls attention to itself, and stands in need of some sort of explanation. No dramatic gesture is self-evident or intrinsically justified; it needs speech to round it out and give it public meaning. Without speech a disobedient act must necessarily appear mute, idiosyncratic, deviant. Without speech disobedience cannot be civil. Thus Thoreau could regard John Brown's raid as a civil act; for, despite its violence, the act was publicly explained by Brown, in his own lean and simple words. He acted always in "broad daylight . . . conspicuous to all parties, with a price set upon his head, going into a courtroom on his way and telling what he had done ... " (Thoreau, 1893c: 415). Had Brown acted clandestinely and anonymously, he would have been no better than Mirabeau the highwayman; yet his willingness and ability to speak made his actions qualitatively different from the common criminal's mute and secretive ways. It was this ability to articulate reasons for acting that Thoreau admitted in John Brown, as well as in Wendell Phillips, the "patrician agitator." [17] Brown, Thoreau tellingly remarked, "could afford to lose his Sharp's rifles, while he retained his faculty of speech—a Sharp's rifle of infinitely surer and longer range" (Thoreau, 1893c: 427). [18] Speech illuminates action by publicly revealing the content of the actor's conscience. Disobedience may be conceived in the privacy of individual conscience, but it acquires its public or civil dimension through speech.

Public disobedience, made civil through speech, is more than a medium for openly revealing one's private convictions; it may also be an instrument of political education. Thoreau declared that in refusing to pay his poll tax and going to jail, "I am doing my part to educate my fellow countrymen now." The lesson is moral rather than material; he is not concerned with tracing the course of his dollar but with "trac[ing] the effects of my allegiance" (Thoreau, 1893c: 380-381). He is no whiggish pedagogue, instilling in his readers a respect for property; he is indifferent to that. But if his fellow townsmen believe that giving a portion of one's property, in the form of taxes, is tantamount to positive consent or even tacit assent, then he will demonstrate his opposition in terms that they can understand. Thoreau withholds his taxes because that is the gesture that others, more mindful of property than he, can readily comprehend. But once he has their attention, he takes pains to indicate that it is not the money that is important, but what (in their Lockean-liberal vocabulary) it represents, that concerns him. In this way he attempts to dramatize an issue, to expose its contradictions, and to persuade others to see the issue in a similar light. Such a symbolic act of disobedience may serve to awaken the sleeping majority, if for no other reason than that the government's response, especially if it be mute and violent, can demonstrate "that what was called order was confusion, what was called justice, injustice, and that the best was deemed the worst" (Thoreau, 1893c: 443). In short, moral and political lessons are best taught by dramatic example.

A civilly disobedient act may also set a precedent by suggesting a course of action for others to follow. Yet Thoreau is mindful of the difficulty in persuading others to join him, even though they recognize "in principle" a right of revolution. "All men," he laments, "recognize the right of revolution ... when [the government's] tyranny or its inefficiency are great and unendurable. But almost all say that such is not the case now" (Thoreau, 1893c: 360). As long as slaves and Abolitionists remain a minority, no matter how just their cause, the right of revolution is not their right. Thoreau realizes that the prospects of massive disobedience are dim, especially if one counsels such action on moral grounds rather than economic interests. Nevertheless, one should act *as if* all men are moral and that, once an individual has set an example, other men will follow. Every individual, that is, should act under the ethnical pretense that he is the sole arbiter of political morality.[19] One can only set an exemplary precedent; one need not force others to follow it.

Yet acting for men, in this sense, does not amount to representing them. In moral matters one man cannot represent another. Moral choice is the prerogative of the individual, and each of us must make his own decisions in matters of conscience. At one point Thoreau shudders to think what his representatives in Congress actually represent; then he wonders whether John Brown might have been his representative at Harper's Ferry, but he interrupts this reverie abruptly by declaring, "No, he was not our representative in any sense. He was too fair a specimen to represent the likes of us." John Brown could not represent Thoreau and other able-bodied Northerners of similar sentiment, for they could represent themselves. "Who, then, were his constituents? If you read his words, you will find out" (Thoreau, 1893c: 427). He represented only those who were unable to act and speak for themselves—the slaves of the South. The aim of Brown's abolitionist activity was to free the slaves, who could then represent themselves and would require no one to act on their behalf. Men cannot be moral until they are free.

Thoreau's conception of political action remains highly individualistic. He appears to have as much in common with some modern existentialists as with the Presocratics, although he defies any easy categorization. His emphasis upon individual freedom of choice, individual responsibility, and public commitment is summed up in his conviction that one lives and acts in the present. A man is bound, he says, to do "only what belongs to himself and the hour" (Thoreau, 1893c: 381). This is not a call to selfish hedonism or withdrawal, but to participation and responsibility. This sense of individual responsibility begets a certain kind of impatience. It is an impatience that makes one reluctant to wait for the machinery of state or society to "adjust" itself or to remedy its own evils; for the ways of the state "take too much time, and a man's life will be gone" (Thoreau, 1893c: 368). A good man will do more than wait: he will speak and act as his conscience bids him.

Civil disobedience, as Thoreau conceives of it, cannot be justified through recourse to traditional liberal principles—that is, to natural law and natural right, expediency and utility, and so on. Its justification turns ultimately upon a conception of action which is foreign to the liberal temper. Given the privative liberal conception of political action, its transformation of the public sphere into a market-place of interests, and its radical separation of speech and action,[20] it is little wonder that Thoreau's thoughts seemed out of season in his own time. His almost-classical conception of political action remains unseasonable, if not unrealistic and irrational, in our day. Thoreau, we are told, was a romantic with no appreciation of the hard realities of American political life; his willful disregard of the "group-basis" of American politics, and his insistence on freeing himself from associational ties, is taken as ample evidence of his irrationality and political naiveté.[21] His emphasis on principled action is out of phase with liberal democracy's elevation of "life without principle" into the epitome of democratic rationality.[22] His conception of political action in general, and civil disobedience in particular, is not streamlined enough to ensure success in a liberal polity where success constitutes the prime criterion of justification. Our aims ought to be suited to our grasp, our ends fitted to our meagre means, our theories made to "correspond" to the facts of political (or apolitical) life.[23] The "costs" of participation in Thoreauvian terms are too high; political action on his terms requires too much time and energy. The point of action should not be to change the world so much as to *use* it—to turn its vices into unintended benefits, its meanness into a "functional equivalent" of virtue, its various forms of violence into surrogates for authority (Arendt, 1963: 101-104; Wolin, 1960: 294-305; Schaar, 1970). Thoreau willfully fails on every count.

If the foregoing is true—if, that is, Thoreau's justification of civil disobedience relies ultimately upon a conception of political action that is out of touch with liberal realities—perhaps we should look elsewhere for some mode of justification which exhibits a better "fit" with the realities of present-day America. This, at least, is the assumption which informs the current search for "realistic" ways of justifying civil disobedience. I turn now to an examination of one of these approaches.

IV. THE SOCIAL FUNCTIONS OF CIVIL DEVIANCE

Social scientists today often speak of "systems," which have "struc-tures" and which perform specifiable "functions" through the agencies of "roles," and so on. "System" is conceived in different ways by different social scientists. One variation on the theme stresses consensus, equilibrium, etc., and is most often associated with Talcott Parsons. Another, which is highly critical of the Parsonian approach, stresses conflict and change. The latter is associated with Ralf Dahrendorf (1958, 1959) and Louis Coser (1956, 1967), among others. The former (Parsonian) image of social systems I shall call the "consensus" model, the latter the "conflict" model. My main concern here will be with the conflict model of society.

Put very crudely, the conflict model views society as a functionally interrelated system of potentially conflicting roles, groups, and sub-systems. For a system to persist over time, some provision must be made for accommodating change without losing the thread of social continuity; otherwise the system would disintegrate (definitionally, at least). Conflict is thought to be inevitable. But this is all to the good, since conflict is usually (though neither always nor necessarily) beneficial, "on the whole" and "in the long run." In other words, conflict may prove to be "functional" for the social system. Various types of conflict may, as Coser (1956: chs. 4, 5) has suggested, actually strengthen the social system by enhancing the strength and status of its constituent groups. Conflict can help define the various roles, rules, and relationships within a social system or sub-system.

What is true of conflict is also true of the related notion of "deviance." Conflict and deviance are both "out of bounds." Yet we can know where the boundaries of acceptable social behavior lie only if some individual or group willfully or unwittingly steps across them. When that happens, the deviant person or group is subjected to the collective disapproval of his fellows. Such disapprobation serves not only as a warning to other potential deviants, but also allows non-deviants to reaffirm shared rules and norms of social behavior. In effect, deviance sets the outer limits of normalcy; it settles the boundaries. Seen from the systemic perspective of the social scientist, various forms of deviance are invaluable or even necessary for the continued functioning of the system.

This perspective on deviance was not originally American, although it is now firmly established as an important field of American social science. The earliest cogent formulations of the sociology of deviance came from two turn-of-the-century European sociologists, Georg Simmel in Germany and Emile Durkheim in France. Although Simmel examined the effects of group conflict and Durkheim dealt with anomie and deviance, both shared a similar perspective and reached congruent conclusions. The most important of these was that "deviant" behavior is not necessarily harmful to society but may indeed be positively beneficial or "functional."

Durkheim's celebrated distinction between the "normal" and the "pathological" in social behavior remains the most explicit formulation of this general thesis. In the *Rules of Sociological Method* (first published in 1895), Durkheim (1964: 63-64) remarks that "if it is true that all that is normal is useful, without being necessary, it is *not* true that all that is useful is norm. . . . The idea of utility is broader than that of normality." Consider crime, for example, as a broad category of deviant social behavior. No society has ever been free of criminal activity. Viewed historically, the presence of crime is the rule rather than the exception, and may therefore be regarded as "normal" from the sociologist's perspective. "To classify crime among the phenomena of normal sociology," says Durkheim (1964: 67), "is not to say that it is an inevitable, although regrettable phenomenon, due to the incorrigible wickedness of men; it is to affirm that it is a factor in public health, an integral part of all healthy societies." Criminality is defined by the "collective conscience" *(conscience collective)* of the society. Whenever a crime is committed, the community's collective conscience is affronted, and its members are given an opportunity to collectively express shock, horror, dismay and general disapprobation. Crime, in other words, provides the impetus as well as the opportunity for a collective reaffirmation of group norms. In this way deviance fosters a sense of group solidarity and is, from the vantage of the dispassionate observer, "functional" for the collectivity at large.

Over the long term, crime or deviance (Durkheim makes no distinctions between the two) may also assist the "evolution" of morality. What is deemed criminal or deviant in one time and place may even be considered praiseworthy in another. "How many times," he proclaims enthusiastically, one kind of deviance "is only an anticipation of future morality—a step toward what will be." An individual or a group condemned as "deviant" in one time may nevertheless be exonerated or even honored by a latter age, whose moral sentiments he may have anticipated. This, Durkheim believed, had been the case with Socrates:

> According to Athenian law, Socrates was a criminal, and his condemnation was no more than just. However, his crime, namely the independence of his thought, rendered a service not only to humanity but to his country. It served to prepare a new morality and faith which the Athenians *needed,* since the traditions by which they had lived until then were no longer in harmony with the current conditions of life. Nor is the case of Socrates unique; it is reproduced periodically in history. It would never have been possible to establish the freedom of thought we now enjoy if the regulations prohibiting it had not been violated (Durkheim, 1964: 71).

The idea that deviance may actually provide a positive service for society was adopted and elaborated by American social scientists. George

Herbert Mead's (1918) work in this genre remains influential today. More recently, Robert Merton (1957), Louis Coser (1956, 1967), Albert Cohen (1966), Kai T. Erikson (1959, 1966), and others have developed many of the insights and implications of this thesis. Today the systematic study of the functions of social deviance is an established and respected branch of American social science.

The moral and political implications of the sociology of deviance are far-reaching with regard to civil disobedience. For if one regards acts of civil disobedience as being in some sense "deviant," it then follows that one can study, explain, and perhaps even justify them in much the same way that one would analyze any other kind of deviant social behavior. Durkheim (1964: 70-73), in his discussion of Socrates, implies as much; Merton (1957: 182-183) and Coser (1967: 124-126, 132-133) have made the point explicitly. Protest, resistance, dissent and disobedience may be designated as deviant activities, although not in any necessarily pejorative sense. Indeed, insofar as such deviance proves "functional" for the system at large, it may be praiseworthy.

In what follows I propose to explore some of the political and ethical implications of viewing civil disobedience as "civil deviance," that is, as a form of potentially functional social deviance. Accordingly, the remainder of this essay will address three main questions. First, what are the purported functions of deviant activity in general, and civil deviance in particular? Second, what are some of the moral assumptions and implications of this functionalist standpoint? And third, what criticisms might be leveled against them?

Before taking up these questions directly, however, one point needs to be clarified at the outset. Most analysts of deviance explicitly disclaim any ethical or "normative" intentions for their work. They claim that the study of the social functions of deviance is empirically descriptive rather than morally evaluative or prescriptive. Merton (1957: 368), for example, insists that viewing deviance and nonconformity from a functionalist perspective represents ". . . not a moral but a functional judgment, not a statement in ethical theory but a statement in sociological theory." Many social scientists claim merely to describe what they find, and with the aid of theories, to systematically interrelate their findings. Yet their theoretical schemas *do* have moral and political implications, whether direct or indirect. As Charles Taylor (1967: 30) notes, a "given set of functional relations defines certain dimensions in which the phenomena can vary; a given framework therefore affirms some dimensions of variation and denies others." A functionalist framework does in fact "secrete a certain value position . . . [It] gives us, as it were, the geography or range of phenomena, it tells us how they can vary, where are the major dimensions of variation. But since we are dealing with matters which are of great importance to human beings a map will have, as it were, its own built-in value-slope."[24] In other words, "a given dimension of variation will usually determine for itself how we are to judge of good and bad, because of its relation to obvious human wants and needs" (Taylor, 1967: 40).

Thus when the sociologist posits a shared human need—for example, that men need to have social rules clarified from time to time—and if the rule-breaker unwittingly serves that wider social need by showing others where the boundaries lie, then he performs a positive service even as he errs. If the ongoing system requires the occasional clarification or modification of its norms, and if one accepts the ethical primacy of "society," then the conclusion follows that the rule-breaking deviant should not be unstintingly condemned. Indeed, he may deserve our thanks. In this manner the functionalist framework "can be said to distribute the onus of argument in a certain way. It is thus not neutral" (Taylor, 1967: 56-57). And so we may, with some slight exaggeration, treat sociological functionalism as a "moral" doctrine, despite the disclaimers of its practitioners. Let me return now to the three questions I posed earlier.

What are the functions of social deviance in general, and civil deviance in particular?

One function is essentially psychological. Civil deviance, as a highly visible form of symbolic activity, is emotive and expressive; as such, it provides a "safety valve," a means of dissipating potentially cumulative and dangerous frustrations, aggressions, etc., in a relatively harmless way. Civil deviance is, on a larger scale, the functional equivalent to what some would call a "good cry": it dissipates pent-up emotions. To this degree civil deviance is therapeutic, a form of political psychodrama. As one participant-observer has remarked, "The Negro has many pent-up resentments and latent frustrations. He has to get them out. . . . If his repressed emotions do not come out in these nonviolent ways, they will come out in ominous expressions of violence." One need not tell Blacks to "get rid of your discontent," but to see to it "that this normal and healthy discontent [is] channelized through the creative outlet of nonviolent direct action." These words might have been written by a psychologist or a sociologist, but they were not: they belong to the late Martin Luther King (1969: 82). This adoption of an essentially social scientific notion (latent hostility in search of a symbolic outlet) by a civil rights activist may suggest something about the manner in which supposedly neutral social-scientific concepts find their way into "normative" political discourse. That this vocabulary lends itself so readily to such usage may suggest that it was heavily weighted with moral import to begin with, and that political activists often see possibilities that escape social scientists: they know a justificatory argument when they see one.

A second function of deviance, to which I alluded before, is essentially adjudicative: it serves to clarify the often ill-defined boundary between normalcy and deviance. As Kai Erikson (1966: 196) suggests, ". . . deviant persons often supply an important service to society by patrolling the outer edges of group space and by providing a contrast which gives the rest of the community some sense of their own territorial identity." Similarly, Coser (1967: 116-117) notes that any "definition of what is considered normal in the group takes place with reference to what is considered deviant, and morality is given its content through the contrast provided by that which is not moral." He detects a "dialectical relationship," viz., that "normalcy can hardly be perceived except against the ground of deviance; to be 'good' makes sense only in relation to being 'bad'." Moreover, he says, "Moral indignation against deviants serves to purge the righteous from a sense of their own sins and . . . helps sustain their moral identity." It is only "against the ground of criminal deviance that the righteous achieve the comforting affirmation of their normality." An interesting, if ominous, example of this phenomenon may be found in the recent "flag fad," when thousands of Americans displayed flag-emblems and automobile bumper-stickers with "patriotic" messages emblazoned in fluorescent red, white and blue. ("America—Love It or Leave It," seems a perennial favorite. Interestingly, the sentiment it expresses—that a citizen unwilling to assent to the dictates of the majority has little choice but to emigrate—might have come straight out of Locke's *Second Treatise.*) This "protest in reverse" was meant to show, as one man put it, "where the real Americans stand." It is meant, said another, to be a "protest against protestors." It provides an opportunity for President Nixon's "silent majority" to express its collective contempt for those whom former Attorney General Kleindeinst calls "ideological criminals" (Newsweek, 1969; Life, 1969; Drew, 1969). In collectively castigating all "civil deviants," members of the so-called silent majority are able to reaffirm their patriotism as they see it. Civil deviance may be "functional" or socially useful insofar as it provides the impetus for a collective reaffirmation of social norms. Far from weakening political allegiance, civil deviance—especially if carried on in a highly visible manner by a relatively small number of deviants—may actually enhance and strengthen sentiments of allegiance and patriotism. Or, in the language of functional analysis, civil deviance may make "manifest" what had previously remained "latent."

More positively, civil deviance may serve yet a third function. For it may serve not only to collectively reaffirm majority sentiments, but also to articulate new sentiments among frustrated but inarticulate minorities, giving them a sense of identity, purpose and solidarity. And in helping to forge a *group* out of a previously inchoate and unorganized mass, acts of civil deviance may prove to be "functional" for the system in the long run, for several reasons. One reason is that organized groups (as opposed, say, to spontaneously acting individuals) tend to "behave" in a "predictable" way; that is, they will seek to maximize their utility in a "rational" manner, which entails: modulating their demands, making them more concrete (or "pragmatic"), more limited, more specific, less "ideological" and more "realistic" than before.[25] Also, organized groups require leaders, and leaders tend to be more flexible and adaptable than do followers (Coser, 1967: 128-132). Thus excessive demands are not made upon the system, which can then accommodate the limited demands that are made. The result is "incremental" or "piecemeal" social and political change, which comes about through the proper "mix" of "consensus" and "cleavage."[26] Conflict and deviance are types of cleavage, and may indirectly promote consensus by clearing the air, getting the issues out in the open, testing the relative strength of the interested parties, providing the impetus for coalition, garnering support, and so on.[27] Each group then having determined its strength and its position vis-à-vis other groups, bargaining and compromise become possible. Acts of civil deviance may spark reassessment, realignment and readjustment within the system at large. As examples of this phenomenon one might cite the Suffragettes, the early labor movement, and the civil rights protests in the American South.

A fourth and closely related function of civil deviance stresses its creative possibilities. Roger Nett (1968: 412-413) has suggested that "Such traditional questions as 'how is conformance brought about and maintained?' may, in social control theory, be misdirected." For such questions "carry unanalyzed assumptions concerning the nature and desirability of conformity . . . ." The secret of successfully "regulating a society," he says, "is to tap, organize and adapt its creative strength." In the end, "the problem of ordering a society becomes one of utilizing the vital element—deviation—in a social-organizational context." He asserts that deviance is a functional requisite for any ongoing system, since "societies are brought to ruin by conformers rather than deviators." Conformers regularly "fail to revitalize society and sustain a healthy social organization. Under conformer dominance, institutions lose their vitality. . . ." The "genius of democratic social organization," he concludes, resides "in its utilization of ... deviation ... within its organizational context." Deviants ought to be tolerated, for they are "potentially productive." Only deviants "can introduce fundamentally new ways into the culture, since the introduction of new ways is deviation." In a similar vein, two political scientists, the late V. O. Key and Karl Deutsch, stress the "creativity" of deviance, while playing down any sense of idealism or responsibility on the part of the "deviant." Key (1961: 554-555) maintains that

> Deviants ... play a critical role in the preservation of the vitality of a democratic order as they urge alterations and modifications better to achieve the aspirations of men. Hence the fundamental significance of freedom of speech and agitation. Those activists closest to the core of power may hesitate to assume the risks of political entrepreneurship, but, others, with less to lose [sic!], may by their efforts gradually make the endeavor that is not 'practical politics' today feasible tomorrow.

Both Key and Deutsch write from a "systemic" perspective. Yet while Key's master metaphor is that of a market system, Deutsch's is that of a communications system. Nevertheless, both reach similar conclusions. Deutsch (1966: 173-174) remarks that

> Very serious challenges to the functioning of a society or state ... may have only those solutions that are fairly unlikely to be discovered by means of the standardized and accepted memories, habits, preferences, and culture patterns existing in the society. If such solutions are found soon enough to be of political significance, they may be more likely to be found by some deviant members of the community—by persons whose memories, habits, or viewpoints may differ significantly from those of most other groups in their community or culture and who may have fewer habits and interests to sacrifice [sic!] in identifying themselves with new ideas and new patterns of behavior.

One ethical and political prescription implied in these functionalist arguments now appears to be fairly explicit. The systemic or functionalist perspective sustains the classical liberal argument for toleration. To some ill-defined degree, deviants ought to be tolerated; they should be given, in J. S. Mill's phrase, "freedom to point out the way." Deviance may disclose functional alternatives. In the language of another age, Mill makes an argument not far removed from the functionalist arguments presented above:

> When the opinions of masses of merely average men are everywhere ... becoming the dominant power, the counterpoise and

corrective to that tendency would be the more pronounced individuality of those who stand on the higher eminences of thought. It is in these circumstances most especially, that exceptional individuals, instead of being deterred, should be encouraged in acting differently from the mass. In other times there was no advantage in their doing so, unless they acted not only differently but better. In this age, the mere example of *non-conformity, the mere refusal to bend the knee to custom, is itself a service.* Precisely because the tyranny of opinion is such as to make eccentricity a reproach, it is desirable, in order to break through that tyranny, that people should be eccentric. . . . That so few now dare to be eccentric marks the chief danger of the time (Mill, 1951: 166-167).

Unlike Mill, who stipulated that the deviant "must not make himself a nuisance to other people" (Mill, 1951: 153), the functionalists are bound by no such gentlemanly scruples. From the functionalist point of view, not only "nuisances" but all manner of deviant and even bellicose actors may serve the social system. Even violence may prove to be "functional" (Coser, 1967). Mill shares with the functionalists a utilitarian orientation; and, while he might have agreed with Durkheim that "the idea of utility is broader than normality," he probably would not wish to press the idea quite as far as the functionalists have done, to include "knavery, skulduggery, cheating, unfairness, crime, sneakiness, malingering, cutting corners, immorality, dishonesty, betrayal, graft, corruption, wickedness, and sin—in short, deviance" (Cohen, 1966: 1). Even if we concede such differences, the orientation is remarkably similar. Whatever else they may have been, the English Utilitarians were gentlemen at heart, and could never quite bring themselves to recognize some of the more bizarre implications of their position. Social scientists of a functionalist persuasion, proclaiming their "neutrality" in moral matters, have, however, been less hesitant to recognize the full range of possibilities entailed by this orientation.

The updated utilitarian perspective of functionalism would thus appear to offer unique possibilities for the justification of civil deviance (Power, 1972). For if it is true that deviance may generally contribute to the viability of the ongoing social system, it follows that so long as one values "society"—as no doubt most of us do, at some vague and visceral level—then whatever contributes to or enhances its existence is to be regarded with tolerance if not approbation. Up to this point I have attempted to argue this "functionalist" position as briefly and as persuasively as I could. There is much to recommend this perspective, and I find myself almost persuaded by it. Almost—but not quite. For there remain a number of objections to be made against some of its ethical implications. Let me enumerate some of these objections.

First of all, viewing civil disobedience as a form of deviance, even "functional" deviance, blinds us to what is *unique* about this kind of action. This perspective is not only limiting; it is also levelling, for no real distinctions are made (nor, given the framework, are any possible) between different kinds of action. For example, civil disobedience is, on this view, fairly indistinguishable from public drunkenness—both are public, illegal, and deviant. When we pass a drunkard on the street, we supposedly reaffirm our own commitment to sobriety. Similarly, when the proverbial "decent, law-abiding citizen" observes or reads about sit-ins, protest marches, and other acts of civil deviance he is afforded an opportunity to reaffirm his own "decency" and commitment to "law and order." Both kinds of deviant activities may thus serve to strengthen the normative framework of society.

Yet surely this conceptual net is not sufficiently fine to permit our making some crucial distinctions. It allows too many different creatures to pass undifferentiated through its wide mesh. A case in point is Durkheim's (1964: 35-36) definition of crime as any and all activities which exhibit "the external characteristic that they evoke from society the particular reaction called punishment.... [E] very punished act [is therefore] a crime." The more sensitive and sophisticated sociologists of deviance have been quick to point out the unduly broad and indiscriminate character of such a conception of criminality. Louis Coser has rightly argued that Durkheim's failure to discriminate among various kinds of deviant social behavior makes *all* deviance "criminal" by fiat. In Durkheim's terms, there is no difference between Jesus' action in "ejecting the merchants from the temple" and the malfeasance of the highway robber. "When all forms of dissent are thus criminal by definition," says Coser (1967: 166-167), "we are in the presence of a [theoretical] system that is ill-equipped to reveal fully the extent to which nonconformity, as distinct from crime, involves the striving toward an alternative moral basis rather than moral deviation." Similarly, Merton (1957: 360) stresses that "nonconformity ... must plainly be distinguished from such other kinds of deviant behavior as (most forms of) crime and delinquency. These kinds of 'deviant behavior' differ structurally, culturally, and functionally." These are welcome and much-needed qualifications.

Yet even in the light of these qualifications, my initial objection can still be sustained. For while the functions of these distinguishable forms of deviance may indeed be different, they nevertheless *are* "functional" from a systemic perspective; they all contribute, in their respective ways, to (say) rule-clarification—even though they serve to clarify *different* rules pertaining to different aspects of the social system. Public drunkenness and political protest may both contribute to the continued functioning of the social system, albeit in different ways. In this respect they are more alike than different. One wonders, then, whether this is really much of an improvement over Durkheim's position, after all.

My second objection is that the functionalist perspective on deviance predisposes one to adopt a posture of uncritical toleration. It creates, that is, a presumption in favor of a "wait and see" attitude. A judgment as to whether a given act or mode of action is functional or dysfunctional has to be retrospective; it cannot ordinarily be prospective, much less predictive in any scientific sense. In the most vulgar sense, this means that success, retrospectively affirmed, is the criterion of functionality; conversely, failure is the mark of dysfunctionality. Thus in the early 1930s, for example, the sociologist could not have predicted whether the violent protests of the Brown Shirts in Germany would be "functional" or not; judgment would have to be suspended, for one could not know in advance that their actions might *not* prove to be socially useful in the long run. The same restrictions and reservations would apply in analyzing Negro civil rights protests in the 1960s. Every individual or group should be equally free, again in Mill's words, "to point out the way"—regardless of where that way might lead. This sort of uncritical toleration—if I may change the metaphor—encourages the most beautiful flowers to grow along with the most odious weeds; and, as any gardener knows, in an untended garden, the weeds seem invariably to win. The functionalist perspective on conflict and deviance supplies us with no criteria for distinguishing flowers from weeds, or nonviolent Negroes from Nazis. To include such evaluative criteria might remove the current bias in favor of winners and against losers.

My third objection is that the functionalist perspective disregards the aims, intentions, motives and reasons—in short, the justifications—tendered by the civil "deviants" themselves. The sociologist is less interested in men's professed reasons (which *may* be "rationalizations" masking some unconscious urge) than in the social-systemic effects of their behavior. This emphasis is reminiscent of the Utilitarians, who stressed the social consequences of individual conduct, rather than the reasons which subtend men's actions. As Bentham (1823: 102) remarked with characteristic bluntness, "If [motives] are good or bad, it is only on account of their *effects*." Even Mill, critical as he was of Bentham, held that "the motive has nothing to do with the morality of the action."[28] The corollary of this proposition is that conscience doesn't count; it is, in Bentham's phrase, "a thing of fictitious existence" (Wolin, 1960: 341). Thus one's reasons for acting are deemed irrelevant; it hardly matters *why* one acts, for only the consequences really count. For this reason the professed aims and justifications of civil deviants may be ignored. The element of *speech*—of giving *reasons* to explain, justify, persuade and educate—is factored out of this functionalist equation, just as it had been excluded from consideration in Paley's market-model of morality. In the end, justifying civil deviance is possible only in "systemic" terms that may well be unintelligible or irrelevant to the "deviants" themselves—and, not least, to the wider audience to whom their actions are presumably addressed.

My fourth objection is closely related to the third. The systemic perspective effectively ignores *individuals,* who become "role-occupants" or are considered noteworthy only insofar as they are members of a group. For example, Merton (1957: 357) stresses that ". . . conformist and noncomformist behavior can be adequately *described,* to say nothing of being adequately *analyzed,* only if this behavior is related to the membership groups and non-membership groups taken as frames of normative and evaluative reference." This methodological injunction entails certain consequences, practical as well as theoretical. As Sheldon Wolin (1960: 385) notes,

> A method dictates a principle of selection; it groups relevant data and ignores others; some phenomena are admitted, others excluded. When these ideas are transferred to social theory, they tend to support the aggregate and denigrate the individual. The aggregate or the collective is to social theory what relevant facts are to method; *pari passu,* the antisocial or unintegrated individual falls under the same suspicion as an irrelevant fact.

While it is often true that individual civil "deviants" do self-consciously act as representatives of some group or other—as Martin Luther King acted for Negroes, for example—this is not always the case. It was not true of Thoreau's act of civil disobedience: for he not only sought to disassociate himself from groups which he had "never signed onto," but to act alone, if need be, as a "majority of one," an independent moral agent free of group commitments and group interests.

To the group-oriented social scientist, then, Thoreau necessarily remains an enigma; he is unclassifiable, which amounts to saying that he is perverse, idiosyncratic, or perhaps deranged. Indeed, a man who acts at the urging of his own conscience rather than the "collective conscience" of a group, may be dangerous. The Hobbesian spectre of the masterless man still haunts much of contemporary social science.[29] The system at large is presumed to be "safe" insofar as most men exhibit multiple group-affiliations, refrain from making "intense" commitments, eschew "ideology," lapse into apolitical apathy, and sink into a kind of privatistic stupor. And yet, it may be "functional" for *some few* individuals to deviate, provided that they belong to (or fall under the de facto jurisdiction of) some social group, which will discipline them and make their action predictable. This appears to be the social-scientific counterpart of "a most peculiar characteristic of pluralistic democracy, namely the combination of tolerance for the most diverse social groups and extreme intolerance for the idiosyncratic individual" (Wolff, 1965: 37).

The supporting argument for all this proceeds along these lines: America is a pluralistic society composed of various groups, associations, parties, interests, etc. The group is the focal point of social and political life; it therefore should be the main focus of attention in social-scientific inquiry. One question for social scientists to ask is, "How are groups maintained; i.e., how do they manage to exist over time?" Various factors may strengthen the social system's constituent groups. One of these factors is internal deviance within groups. A deviant individual may help strengthen a group with which he is associated (Erikson and Dentler, 1959). And in so doing, his deviant behavior adds, in small measure, to the strength and stability of the system as a whole. This presupposes, however, that the deviant individual does have a reference group with its own established norms and standards of behavior. In short, deviance may be useful or "functional" insofar as it is a group-related activity.

A preoccupation with "usefulness" in its various forms—with means, techniques, methods, tactics, and so on—is so much a part of our present-day political perspective that even would-be advocates of civil disobedience often speak in its idiom. One defender of "useful" or functional civil disobedience has recently reproached Thoreau because "His act is not a *tactic* in a campaign of mass disobedience . . . he scorns any appeal to the *utility* of his act, and he is wholly unmoved by its possible *inexpediency* (as his dismissal of Paley shows)." Thoreau, he concludes, "remains somewhat unconvincing and alien" (Bedau, 1969: 26). And surely this is so, given the underlying assumptions of utilitarian liberalism, a perspective shared by means-minded, "pragmatic" liberals, as well as social scientists of a "functionalist" persuasion.

These considerations suggest yet a fifth objection to the concept of civil deviance. My contention is that the twin notions of "function" and "utility" are covert expressions of a moral posture that stresses the primacy of means, method and technique over moral ends. Thoreau saw this in Paley's utilitarianism, with its emphasis upon "cost," "convenience," and "expediency." Implicit in Paley's doctrine was an ethical gradualism, an emphasis upon piecemeal reform, and a counsel of caution to those whose moral indignation might bid them throw caution to the wind. The ends are to be subservient to the means; what is technically feasible becomes, by default, morally desirable. This is perhaps the most distinctive mark of American liberalism, which has traditionally prided itself on its pragmatic, no-nonsense conception of political action as a matter of technique—as "the art of the possible," whereby ends are reduced to interests, and then fitted to the available means and mechanisms of the political "market."[30] The metaphor of the market may represent the outer limits of the liberal imagination. And perhaps that is why a conception of political action (such as Thoreau's) which stresses the publicness of its ends more than the personal costs or inconvenience of its means, is quite inconceivable within its purview. To this the liberal critic invariably responds that "Thoreau makes the ends justify the means," and lets it go at that. Yet the cliché is confused: what else but the end *could* possibly justify the means? Although the standard liberal rejoinder seems confused, it is nevertheless revealing. For it brings into bold relief the liberal conception of the ethical primacy of means, techniques and procedures.

Perhaps one explanation for the seemingly self-evident plausibility of viewing political action as a matter of means or technique lies in an unexamined conceptual confusion. Like "utility," the term "function" was originally a descriptive and context-dependent means-word. Yet it appears that both terms have effectively been transmuted into prescriptive and context-free end-words. Just as the Utilitarians elevated "utility" into a principle, so the functionalists have in effect done the same thing with "function." Yet the question that astute critics have addressed to the Utilitarians—useful for what?—has not, perhaps, been persistently enough asked of the functionalists.[31] When we are told by the sociologists that civil deviance is or may prove to be "functional," we should inquire: functional for what? or for whom? We should probably receive no more satisfying a response than: "Functional for society and/or its constituent groups." Yet their ethical referent—"society"—is intractibly vague and emotive. Like the Utilitarian's "happiness," the functionalist's "society" is, in Friedrich Waismann's instructive phrase, a "hat-doffing" word: it elicits approval, and we acknowledge it in a vague and polite way, without bothering to question its meaning. That it is generally not questioned does not mean that it is not questionable. For we should surely want to know what *kind* of society is worth defending; surely the fact that it "works" is not a sufficient reason for contributing to its continued functioning, whether as a "civil deviant" or in some other capacity.

While the pragmatic liberal asks about the costs of disobedience,[32] the Thoreauvian radical asks whether one should tolerate that which one finds intolerable, regardless of the "costs" incurred. What price silence?

Thoreau strikes a responsive, if "irrational," chord in most of us. Yet, given the liberal conception of political action with which we have been inculcated, we do not know what to do. It may not be too far-fetched to suggest that Thoreau represents the bad conscience of American liberalism, and that is why liberals hardly know what to do with him. He is a skeleton in the closet of their collective conscience.

My sixth objection to the idea of "civil deviance" concerns the implications of regarding individuals or minorities as deviant with respect to the majority. There appears to be something rather smug, as Thoreau recognized, in supposing that the larger aggregate supplies an ethical yardstick or standard for evaluating all political action. Is it not at least possible that the majority may itself be "deviant" in its failure to adhere to its own professed values? It has been assumed that acts of civil deviance are meant to break radically with the past, to create new values or to give new meaning to old ones. Civil deviance is taken to be action de novo—different, critical of the past, "creative" (Nett, 1968; Deutsch, 1966), "striving toward an alternative moral basis" (Coser, 1967). Yet the history of civil disobedience in America not only fails to sustain this interpretation, but in many cases refutes it. The extent to which civil disobedience may be "conservative" has rarely been appreciated. For civilly disobedient activists often wish to convey the message that the majority itself is "deviant"—that it has failed to square its political practices with its own professed values. This was the spirit in which civil disobedience was practiced in the South: it served to remind Americans that racial discrimination was incompatible with our almost ritualistic incantations of equality, of freedom to vote, and so on. Far from advocating a radical break with our ideals and moral traditions, these activists insisted that we hark back to these ideals, that we take them seriously and attempt, in short, to practice what we preach. Civil disobedience may represent, in the American context at least, an attempt to bring into sharp relief the discontinuity of ideals and practices. It seeks to portray, in dramatic and direct form, the "deviance" of a society that can preach high ideals while practicing moral abominations. Thoreau saw this clearly, as did Van Wyck Brooks a half-century later. In America, Brooks (1915: 7) said, "One finds this frank acceptance of twin values which are not expected to have anything in common: on the one hand a quite unclouded, quite unhypocritical assumption of transcendent theory ('high ideals'); on the other, a simultaneous acceptance of catchpenny realities." Yet, strangely enough, the sociologists of deviance have never considered the possibility that a whole society may be deviant and that, as regards mutually acknowledged ideals and values, the "deviants" may in fact be the conformists. Deviant is as deviant does.

My seventh objection is not easy to articulate, for it concerns metaphor, and metaphors are by their very nature not amenable to linguistic reformulation and criticism. The language of social science, like any other, is replete with metaphors and images of various kinds. Sociological functionalism exhibits a special penchant, it seems, for organic and mechanical metaphors; more precisely, the "consensus" model of society tends to employ metaphors drawn from biology, while the "conflict" perspective evinces a special fondness for metaphors drawn from mechanics. (One might note in passing the affinities between this latter perspective and Madison's tenth *Federalist.*) One of the most common mechanical metaphors is that of the steam-valve or safety-valve, and related images like "pressure." Thus Coser (1956: 48), for example, suggests that

> Social systems provide for specific institutions which serve to drain off hostile and aggressive sentiments. These safety-valve institutions help to maintain the system by preventing otherwise probably conflict or by reducing its disruptive effects. They provide substitute objects upon which to displace hostile sentiments, as well as means of abreaction. Through these safety valves, hostility is prevented from turning against its original object.

This seems quite unexceptionable, on the face of it; indeed, we say as much when we speak of someone's "letting off steam," or "venting his hostility." Yet metaphors do have consequences inasmuch as they inform our language, and hence our ways of thinking and acting. As George Eliot said so succinctly in *Middlemarch*, "All of us, grave or light, get our thoughts entangled in metaphors, and act fatally on the strength of them." What, then, might be the implications of viewing an institution or a practice—in this case, civil deviance—as a social safety-valve?

Since a single story may be worth a hundred hypotheses, let me relate an instance in which the safety-valve metaphor was vividly used and heatedly criticized in an actual political situation. Following the Cambodian invasion and its calamitous domestic aftermath, President Nixon called a press conference. When asked about the upcoming demonstrations in the capitol, the President replied that he was "in favor" of protest, because it was a useful "safety valve" which allowed pent-up emotions and hostilities to be symbolically and harmlessly dissipated (Times, 1970a: 8). The next day in Washington, David Dellinger objected to the President's safety-valve metaphor and its implications. At the macro- or structural level, the underlying idea of a safety valve is that the structure of the machine of which it is a part is fundamentally sound and needs no basic changes. At the micro- or psychological level, the safety-valve metaphor tends to demean and trivialize one's actions. Political protests and infantile tantrums are functionally equivalent, for both facilitate the release of tensions, pressures, steam and hot air (Times, 1970b: 24). The objections raised by Dellinger against the President's safety-valve metaphor seem to coincide with several of my reservations about the functionalist approach to civil deviance. For the steam-valve metaphor fails to distinguish between different kinds of actions; it is uncritically tolerant and smugly patronizing; it fails to take into account the reasoned arguments of the actors involved, i.e., it is deaf to the speech that might justify, explain and educate; and it celebrates the continued existence of the "system" without taking a second look at that system itself. This coincidence between Dellinger's criticisms and mine may be due to the fact that the objects of our criticisms—steam valves and social systems—are metaphors. They are, moreover, metaphors which obfuscate as often as they clarify, and darken as much as they illuminate.

Although I have by no means exhausted the list of objections that might be raised against the ethical and political implications of the functionalist perspective on "civil deviance," I shall mention one last objection—one that is, to my mind, perhaps most important of all. Those who would justify civil disobedience on functional grounds tend to do so in terms *other* than the "deviants" themselves might find acceptable. For example, it may (retrospectively) be argued that the Abolitionists performed a positive service for the American economic system. The prime consideration, on this reckoning, should be *not* that slavery was morally abhorrent but that it was a dysfunctional anachronism.[33] The activity of the Abolitionists is justified, in retrospect, because we can now see that it hastened the demise of an obsolete and inefficient economic institution. Slavery, with its pool of cheap labor, slowed the introduction of still cheaper and more efficient methods of agriculture, e.g., machinery to pick and process cotton. The ethical posture assumed by the Abolitionists is, on this accounting, as irrelevant as it is quaint. For their "real" service was not primarily a moral one, as they had assumed, but a "systemic" service that they never recognized or acknowledged.

Now this may seem plausible and praiseworthy enough, until we consider: What if the abolition of slavery, at this time, had *not* been "functional"? What if it had been, on the contrary, clearly "dysfunctional": should we not then have to count the Abolitionists dangerous or perverse? Given a utilitarian or functionalist framework, we should initially have to answer in the affirmative. Even so, we might wish to introduce other, overriding considerations such as justice or fairness. We might even argue, with Thoreau and Rawls (1962) that the utility or inutility, efficiency or inefficiency, function or dysfunction of a practice or an institution may have little to do with whether it is just or fair. To render justice may result in technical inefficiency, perhaps even social dysfunction and inutility. Yet it does not follow that injustice, or rather an emasculated redefinition of justice, is therefore to be preferred. The "rule of expediency" ought not always apply.

With this last consideration we have come full circle. We find ourselves going back to Thoreau's quarrel with Paley. When one substitutes the newer term "function" for the older concept of "utility," one can readily imagine Thoreau arguing against the ethical and political implications of a thoroughgoing sociological functionalism. Like Paley and the Utilitarians, whose position parallels theirs in so many ways, the functionalists wield some influence over the way men conceive and execute their programs of political action. Our thoughts become entangled in their metaphors. The distribution of emphasis in both these perspectives supports an initial presumption in favor of a certain liberal mode of political action, and militates against the conception or creation of alternative forms of action. This is most clearly illustrated in their justifications of "deviance" from a systemic perspective. To the extent that "civil deviance" proves to be functional (i.e., retrospectively adjudged successful or effective), it is justifiable. But what if slavery, or segregation, or the war in Vietnam *were* "functional" for (say) the economic system of the United States? Thoreau's answer still remains: "[in] those cases to which the rule of expediency does not apply, . . . a people, as well as an individual, must do justice, *cost what it may.*" Even if civil disobedience were "dysfunctional" on a particular occasion, that consideration *by itself* would not be a morally sufficient condition for proscribing resistance. For in the end the decision to disobey is surely as much a moral as an empirical matter—a matter not only of private conscience, but of reasoned conviction and public responsibility.

NOTES

1. Actually, Rossiter is mistaken on two counts: for Locke, "rebellion" is *never* justifiable; nor did he write his *Second Treatise,* as Laslett (1960: 58-79) has shown, to justify the Glorious Revolution. Yet it may well be that colonial Americans *believed* this to have been Locke's purpose, thereby adding to his prestige in America.

2. Locke specifies that "acting contrary to [government's] trust" consists in its intrusion into, or failure to protect the property of its citizens. When a majority of citizens perceive the government's failure to protect their property, they are no

longer obligated to obey that government and the right of revolution becomes operative. My brief account of Locke's conception of political obligation and the attendant right of revolution is, of course, greatly oversimplified. For richer readings of Locke, see Pitkin (1965: 994-997) and Dunn (1969b: 177-186).

3. These themes are ubiquitous in Jefferson's correspondence. In his letter of 3 April 1809, addressed to "The Inhabitants of Albemarle County in Virginia," Jefferson (1892, IX: 250-251) speaks of the "distressing burden" of the political vocation and of his longing for the "repose [of] private life." And in a letter to Dupont de Nemours, dated 2 March 1809, Jefferson (1830, IV: 125-126) likens the political actor to a "prisoner" whose one hope and desire is to "shake off the shackles of power."

4. On Jefferson's antipathy toward the city, see Morton and Lucia White (1962, ch. 2). On the political implications of agrarianism, see McConnell (1953) and Griswold (1948).

5. Paley has sunk into undeserved obscurity. His work deserves to be better known than it presently is. Among the best accounts of Paley's doctrine and its influence is Stephen (1902, I: 405ff.). On the similarities between Paley's and Bentham's utilitarianism, see Stephen (1900, I: ch's. 5, 6) and Halevy (1929). For a synoptic overview, see Barker (1948).

6. Strange as the combination may appear to us today, it was common fare in the latter half of the eighteenth century and well into the nineteenth. On the attempts to combine natural law with utilitarianism, see Sabine (1961: 544) and Gay (1969: 455-460).

7. On the conformitarian implications of utilitarianism, see Dicey (1914: 303-310) and Cole (1934: 45-46). Smith (1954: 410) mistakenly claims that Paley's utilitarianism, unlike Bentham's, "remained individualistic to the core." While it is true that Paley (1785: 423) held that "Every man [shall judge] for himself" in applying to utilitarian calculus in matters of obedience or resistance to government," he added that one may judge wrongly and suffer grievously as a result. Paley's implicit model for moral decision has its roots in the Christian doctrine of free will, wherein each man is "free" to choose God or the devil: but the promised consequences of the wrong choice constrain men in their decisions, predisposing them to make the "correct" choice. Given similar constraints on moral and political decisions, the choice of paths taken by a rational calculator of expediency is virtually a foregone conclusion.

8. And this in spite of Emerson's (1911, VI: 440-441) warning that Thoreau's readers will be misled if they read him literally and without an appreciation of his love of punning, paradox, and other stylistic devices. See also, in this connection, Hyman (1962) and Paul (1958).

9. These passages are strikingly reminiscent of Rousseau's puns on *constitution* in the preface to his *Second Discourse*. Compare Thoreau's playful treatment of "governor" in *Slavery in Massachusetts* (1893c: 390-392).

10. "The systems of the political philosophers achieve their effects in so far as they displace our customary centre of vision and substitute for it a centre from which everything looks new and strange" (Cameron, 1955: 99-100). For an explication and examination of the notion of "paradigm shifts" in political-theoretical perspectives, see Wolin (1968). Thoreau's political essays may be read as attempts to bring about just such "shifts" by skewing language in various ways so as to call into question the tacit assumptions of our thought. This he does not merely by punning and employing various stylistic devices, but also by juxtaposing apparently incongruous concepts in

order to command a "second look" by the reader. Such juxtaposition occurs perhaps most notably in the neologism "civil disobedience."

11. Thoreau's position here is not necessarily "undemocratic." It rather more resembles the Quakers' objection to majority rule: see Beitzinger (1972: 71-73).

12. This does not, however, mean that a collectivity can never be an instrument of the good: "It is truly enough said that a corporation has no conscience; but a corporation of conscientious men is a corporation *with* a conscience" (Thoreau, 1893c: 358). This kind of moral and methodological individualism underlies Thoreau's *pro*-government pleas in *Slavery in Massachusetts* and in *A Plea for Captain John Brown* (Thoreau, 1893c: 404-405, 429, 431).

13. In defending Thoreau against his critics' mistaken charges I do not mean to suggest that I am fully persuaded by Thoreau's arguments. Quite the contrary: I am most skeptical of many of them—especially his reliance on "conscience" and his "whatever-the-costs" perspective. Reservations much like my own can be found in Broad (1952) and Bennett (1966).

14. Thoreau could hardly have foreseen a time like ours, when the funding of schools and the building of highways would arouse public controversy. Yet his lack of foresight in such matters need not detract from the force of his criticism or the validity of his point.

15. In a *Journal* entry dated 26 March 1842 Thoreau (1893d: 350) wrote: "I have no private good unless it be my peculiar ability to serve the *public*." Compare his remarks in *Civil Disobedience* (Thoreau, 1893c: 357).

16. Parrington (1927, II: 411) calls Thoreau an "individual syndicalist"; Madden (1968: 97) remarks outright that "Thoreau, in short, was an anarchist"; and even Kariel, in his otherwise superb analysis of American pluralism, calls Thoreau "the most sustained advocate of anarchism" (Kariel, 1961: 193). Even some anarchists—Count Tolstoy and Emma Goldman among them—have regarded Thoreau as one of their own.

17. On Phillips as agitator, see Hofstadter (1948, ch. 6). Hofstadter's essay provides a useful corrective to the views expressed by Eulau (1962).

18. Thoreau's emphasis on speech—understood not as vulgar rhetoric but as a means of self-disclosure and a complement to action—reveals his debt to the Greeks. For an illuminating discussion of speech and action in their classical senses, see Arendt (1959: 25-27, 158-178).

19. Thoreau's individualist ethic—his emphasis upon individual conscience, choice and responsibility—is reminiscent of Kant's categorical imperative: "Act only according to that maxim by which you can at the same time will that it should become a universal law" (Kant, 1964: 91). Recently, Lynd (1968: 168-169) has argued that American radicalism has been much influenced by Kant, inasmuch as he offered an alternative to Locke. Theodore Parker, William Ellery Channing, Thorstein Veblen and W.E.B. DuBois, among others, explicitly acknowledged their debt to Kant.

20. Consider, for example, the right of free speech. The conditions under which this right applies, in practice, stipulate that speech ceases to be free and protected when it crosses the ill-defined line between "expression" and "advocacy." The latter is suspect because it may lead men to act. Speech can be free, i.e., tolerated, only so long as it remains divorced from action—or rather, from certain kinds of actions, namely those which might disrupt the normal functioning of society.

21. The charge is that, since Thoreau refused to accommodate himself to what passes for the political vocation in the liberal state, he is therefore "apolitical," or perhaps even "antipolitical." See, in particular, Eulau (1962) and Martin (1970: 138).

22. This is not quite true, since political action in the liberal sense is in fact informed by certain principles. I wish only to stress, with Thoreau, the prudential and unheroic character of these principles, e.g., Paley's principle of least effort (the maximization of convenience), the principle of self-interest and the avoidance of pain, etc. For further discussion, see Wolin (1960: 314 f.).

23. It is currently fashionable to espouse "the view that theories of politics should be drawn from the realities of political life," and to denigrate the idea that "the realities of political life should be molded to fit one's theories" (Almond and Verba, 1965: 340). This perspective ignores the possibility that a political system may be instituted and established according to "theoretical" conceptions which, when institutionalized, make "facts" out of "theory" and become an integral part of political education and of our very conception of politics. See, in this connection, Jacobson (1963) and Wolin (1969).

24. Arguments differing from, but compatible with, Taylor's may be found in Braybrooke (1958: 992-1004) and Stretton (1969). See especially the valuable critique of Merton, Dahrendorf and Coser in Stretton (1969: 174-183, 318-325).

25. This would appear to be the "political" counterpart of rationality in a competitive market situation. For a development of themes related to this perspective, see Downs (1957), Buchanan and Tullock (1962), and Braybrooke and Lindblom (1963).

26. "Cleavage" is usually employed as an umbrella concept covering a wide variety of social phenomena, including "deviance" in its various forms. On the systemic functions of cleavage, see Easton (1965: 236-240).

27. This view has not, to be sure, wanted for critics. See especially Kariel (1962), McConnell (1966, ch's. 5, 6), Wolff (1965), Lowi (1967), and Beam (1970).

28. Mill (1951: 22) does add, however, that the motive does have "much [to do] with the worth of the agent." This separation of the moral worth of an action from the agent who performs it, stands in vivid contrast to an older tradition which viewed act and actor as inseparable. Thus Aristotle (1953, Bk. II, ch. 4): "Virtuous actions are not done in a virtuous . . . . way merely because they have the appropriate quality. The *doer* must be in a certain frame of mind when he does them." Even a proto-Utilitarian like Hume (1888, Bk. III, part ii, sec. 1) held that "when we praise any actions, we regard only the motives that produced them, and consider the actions as signs or indications of certain principles in the mind and temper. The external performance has no merit. We must look within to find the moral quality."

29. This fear is particularly evident in social-scientific analyses of totalitarianism and mass society. See the critiques by Euben (1970) and Bramson (1961).

30. This, at any rate, is the way the American political system is characterized by Almond (1956: 398): "The political system is saturated with the atmosphere of the market"—so much so, indeed, that elected leaders may be viewed "as brokers occupying points in the bargaining process." Almond is not merely describing this state of affairs: he is celebrating it. For a critique of the "market" conception of politics, see Tussman (1960, ch. 4).

31. Pointed questions of this sort have been asked about the functionally-oriented voting studies and about "realistic" theories of democracy. See in particular

the essays by Duncan and Lukes, Davis, Goldschmidt, and Walker, in McCoy and Playford (1967). For a synoptic overview and critique, see Bachrach (1967).

32. Paley (1785) still provides the paradigm for this kind of inquiry. For a modern restatement of the Paleyan thesis, see Buchanan and Tullock (1962: 262).

33. A particularly straightforward claim of this kind was advanced by a prominent Marxist historian (Genovese, 1968) in a heated exchange over the "functions" of slavery. He contended "that at certain times throughout history [slavery and servitude] contributed to social development and that the moral case against modern slavery must rest on its being a historical anachronism."

REFERENCES

ALMOND, G. A. (1956) "Comparative political systems," J. of Pol. 18 (August): 391-409.

––– and S. VERBA (1965) The Civic Culture. Boston: Little, Brown.

ARENDT, H. (1959) The Human Condition. New York: Doubleday Anchor.

––– (1963) "What is authority?" in Between Past and Future. New York: Viking.

ARISTOTLE (1953) Ethics. London: Penguin.

BACHRACH, P. (1967) The Theory of Democratic Elitism: A Critique. Boston: Little, Brown.

BAILYN, B. (1967) Ideological Origins of the American Revolution. Cambridge, Mass.: Harvard Univ. Press.

BARKER, E. (1948) "Paley and his political philosophy," in Traditions of Civility. Cambridge: Cambridge Univ. Press.

BEAM, G. D. (1970) Usual Politics: A Critique and Some Suggestions for an Alternative. New York: Holt, Rinehart & Winston.

BEDAU, H. (1969) Civil Disobedience. New York: Pegasus.

BEITZINGER, A. J. (1972) A History of American Political Thought. New York: Dodd, Mead.

BENNETT, J. (1966) "Whatever the consequences." Analysis 26: 83-102.

BENTHAM, J. (1823) The Principles of Morals and Legislation. London: T. Payne & Sons.

BRAMSON, L. (1961) The Political Context of Sociology. Princeton, N.J.: Princeton Univ. Press.

BRAYBROOKE, D. (1958) "The relevance of norms to political description." Amer. Pol. Sci. Rev. 52 (December): 989-1006.

––– and C. E. LINDBLOM (1963) A Strategy of Decision. New York: Free Press.

BROAD, C. D. (1952) "Conscience and conscientious action," in Ethics and the History of Philosophy. London: Routledge & Kegan Paul.

BROOKS, V. W. (1915) America's Coming-of-Age. New York: Huebsch.

BUCHANAN, J. M. and G. TULLOCK (1962) The Calculus of Consent. Ann Arbor: Univ. of Michigan Press.

CAMERON, T. M. (1955) "The justification of political attitudes." Proceedings of the Aristotelian Society, supplmentary vol. XXIX.

COHEN, A. K. (1966) Deviance and Control. Englewood Cliffs, N.J.: Prentice-Hall.

COLE, G.D.H. (1934) Some Relations Between Political and Economic Theory. London: Macmillan.

COSER, L. (1956) The Functions of Social Conflict. New York: Free Press.

––– (1967) Continuities in the Study of Social Conflict. New York: Free Press.

CURTI, M. (1937) "The great Mr. Locke, America's philosopher." Huntington Library Bull. no. 11 (April): 107-151.

DAHRENDORF, R. (1958) "Out of utopia: toward a reorientation of sociological analysis." Amer. J. of Soc. 64 (September): 115-127.

––– (1959) Class and Class Conflict in Industrial Society. Stanford, Calif.: Stanford Univ. Press.

DICEY, A. V. (1914) Lectures on the Relationship Between Law and Public Opinion in England. London: Macmillan.

DOWNS, A. (1957) An Economic Theory of Democracy. New York: Harper & Row.

DREW, E. B. (1969) "Report from Washington." Atlantic Monthly (May): 4-12.

DRINNON, R. (1966) "Thoreau's politics of the upright man," pp. 410-422 in O. Thomas (ed.) Henry David Thoreau: Walden and Civil Disobedience–Authoritative Texts, Background, Criticism. New York: Norton.

DUNN, J. (1969a) "The politics of Locke in England and America," in J. W. Yolton, John Locke: Problems and Perspectives. Cambridge: Cambridge Univ. Press.

––– (1969b) The Political Thought of John Locke. Cambridge: Cambridge Univ. Press.

DURKHEIM, E. (1964) The Rules of Sociological Method. (S. A. Solovay and J. H. Mueller, trans.). New York: Free Press.

EASTON, D. (1965) A Systems Analysis of Political Life. New York: John Wiley.

EMERSON, R. W. (1911) Journals. E. W. Emerson and W. E. Forbes (eds.) Boston: Houghton Mifflin.

ERIKSON, K. T. (1966) Wayward Puritans: A Study in the Sociology of Deviance. New York: John Wiley.

––– and R. A. DENTLER (1959) "The functions of deviance in groups." Social Problems. 7 (Fall): 98-107.

EUBEN, J. P. (1970) "Political science and political silence," pp. 3-58 in P. Green and S. Levinson (eds.) Power and Community: Dissenting Essays in Political Science. New York: Pantheon.

EULAU, H. (1962) "Wayside challenger: some remarks on the politics of Henry David Thoreau," pp. 117-130 in S. Paul (ed.) Thoreau: A Collection of Critical Essays. Englewood Cliffs, N.J.: Prentice-Hall.

GAY, PETER (1969) The Enlightenment: An Interpretation, vol. II. New York: Knopf.

GENOVESE (1968) "An exchange with Staughton Lynd." New York Review, XI (19 December): 36.

GREEN, P. and S. LEVINSON [eds.] (1970) Power and Community: Dissenting Essays in Political Science. New York: Pantheon.

GRISWOLD, A. W. (1948) Farming and Democracy. New York: Harcourt, Brace.

HALEVY, E. (1929) The Growth of Philosophic Radicalism. London: Faber & Faber.

HARTZ, L. (1955) The Liberal Tradition in America. New York: Harcourt, Brace.

HOFSTADTER, R. (1948) The American Political Tradition. New York: Knopf.

HOOK, S. (1964) The Paradoxes of Freedom. Berkeley and Los Angeles: Univ. of California Press.

HUME, D. (1888) In L. A. Selby-Bigge (ed.) A Treatise of Human Nature. Oxford: Clarendon Press.

HYMAN, S. E. (1962) "Henry Thoreau in our time," pp. 23-26 in S. Paul (ed.) Thoreau: A Collection of Critical Essays. Englewood Cliffs, N.J.: Prentice-Hall.

JACOBSON, N. (1963) "Political science and political education." Amer. Pol. Sci. Rev. 63 (December): 1062-1082.

JEFFERSON, T. (1830) In T. J. Randolph (ed.) Memoir, Correspondence, and Miscellanies. Boston: Gray & Bowen.

――― (1892) In P. L. Ford (ed.) Writings. New York: Putnam.

――― (1955) In E. Dumbauld (ed.) The Political Writings of Thomas Jefferson. New York: Liberal Arts Press.

――― (1961) In J. Boyd (ed.) Papers. Vol. XVI. Princeton: Princeton Univ. Press.

KANT, I. (1964) Groundwork of the Metaphysic of Morals. (H. J. Paton, trans.) New York: Harper.

KARIEL, H. (1961) The Decline of American Pluralism. Stanford, Calif.: Stanford Univ. Press.

KEY, V. O. (1961) Public Opinion and American Democracy. New York: Knopf.

KING, M. L. (1969) "Letter from Birmingham jail," in H. Bedau (ed.) Civil Disobedience. New York: Pegasus.

KING, P. and C. B. PAREKH [eds.] (1968) Politics and Experience: Essays Presented to Michael Oakeshott. Cambridge: Cambridge Univ. Press.

LASLETT, P. (1960) Introduction to Locke.

――― and W. G. RUNCIMAN [eds.] (1962) Philosophy, Politics, and Society. Second Series. Oxford: Blackwell.

LEVY, L. W. (1963) Jefferson and Civil Liberties: The Darker Side. Cambridge, Mass.: Harvard Univ. Press.

Life (1969): July 18.

LOCKE, J. (1960) In P. Laslett (ed.) Two Treatises of Government. Cambridge: Cambridge Univ. Press.

LOWI, T. (1967) "The public philosophy: interest-group liberalism." Amer. Pol. Sci. Rev. 61 (March): 5-24.

LYND, S. (1968) Intellectual Origins of American Radicalism. New York: Pantheon.

MADDEN, C. (1968) Civil Disobedience and Moral Law. Seattle: Univ. of Washington Press.

MADISON, J. (1904) In G. Hunt (ed.) Writings. Vol. V. New York: Putnam.

McCONNELL, G. (1953) The Decline of Agrarian Democracy. Berkeley and Los Angeles: Univ. of California Press.

――― (1966) Private Power and American Democracy. New York: Knopf.

McCOY, C. A., AND J. PLAYFORD [eds.] (1967) Apolitical Politics: A Critique of Behavioralism. New York: Crowell.

MARTIN, R. (1970) "Civil disobedience" Ethics 80 (January): 123-139.

MAYO, H. B. (1960) An Introduction to Democratic Theory. New York: Oxford Univ. Press.

MEAD, G. H. (1918) "The psychology of punitive justice." Amer. J. of Soc. 23: 585-92.

MERTON, R. K. (1957) Social Theory and Social Structure. Rev. Edn. New York: Free Press.

MILL, J. S. (1951) "On liberty," in Utilitarianism, Liberty and Representative Government. New York: Dutton.

National Commission on the Causes and Prevention of Violence (1969) To Establish Justice, to Insure Domestic Tranquility: Final Report of the National Commission on the Causes and Prevention of Violence. Washington, D.C.: Government Printing Office.

NETT, R. (1968) "Conformity-deviation and the social control concept," in W. Buckley (ed.) Modern Systems Research for the Behavioral Scientist. Chicago: Aldine.

Newsweek (1969): June 30.

PALEY, W. (1785) Principles of Moral and Political Philosophy. London: Printed by J. Davis.

PARRINGTON, V. L. (1927) Main Currents in American Thought. New York: Harcourt, Brace.

PAUL, S. (1958) The Shores of America: Thoreau's Inward Exploration. Urbana: Univ. of Illinois Press.

——— [ed.] (1962) Thoreau: A Collection of Critical Essays. Englewood Cliffs, N.J.: Prentice-Hall.

PITKIN, H. (1965) "Obligation and consent—I." Amer. Pol. Sci. Rev. 59 (December): 990-999.

POWER, P. F. (1972) "Civil disobedience as functional opposition." J. of Pol. 34 (February): 37-55.

RAWLS, J. (1962) "Justice as fairness," pp. 132-157 in P. Laslett and W. G. Runciman (eds.) Philosophy, Politics, and Society. Second Series. Oxford: Blackwell.

ROSSITER, C. (1963) The Political Thought of the American Revolution. New York: Harcourt, Brace.

SABINE, G. H. (1961) A History of Political Theory. New York: Holt, Rinehart & Winston.

SCHAAR, J. H. (1970) "Legitimacy in the modern state," in P. Green and S. Levinson (eds.) Power and Community: Dissenting Essays in Political Science. New York: Pantheon.

SEYBOLD, H. (1951) Thoreau: The Quest and the Classics. New Haven, Conn.: Yale Univ. Press.

SMITH, W. (1954) "William Paley's theological utilitarianism in America," William and Mary Q. Third series, XI: 402-424.

STEPHEN, L. (1900) The English Utilitarians. London: Duckworth.

——— (1902) English Thought in the Eighteenth Century. London: John Murray.

STRETTON, H. (1969) The Political Sciences. London: Routledge & Kegan Paul.

TAYLOR, C. (1967) "Neutrality in political science," in P. Laslett and W. G. Runciman (eds.) Philosophy, Politics, and Society. Third Series. Oxford: Blackwell.

THOMAS, O. [ed.] (1966) Henry David Thoreau: Walden and Civil Disobedience— Authoritative Texts, Background, Criticism. New York: Norton.

THOREAU, H. D. (1893a) A Week on the Concord and Merrimack Rivers, in H. S. Canby (ed.) Thoreau, Writings. Vol. I. Boston: Houghton Mifflin.

——— (1893b) Walden, in Writings. Vol. II.

——— (1893c) Civil Disobedience and Other Political Essays, in Writings. Vol. IV.

——— (1893d) Journal, in Writings. Vol. VII.

Times (1970a) New York: May 9.

——— (1970b) New York: May 10.

TUSSMAN, J. (1960) Obligation and the Body Politic. New York: Oxford Univ. Press.

WALZER, M. (1970) Obligations. Cambridge, Mass.: Harvard Univ. Press.

WHITE, M. and L. WHITE (1962) The Intellectual Versus the City. Cambridge, Mass.: Harvard Univ. Press.

WOLFF, R. P. (1965) "Beyond tolerance," in R. P. Wolff, B. Moore, Jr., and H. Marcuse, A Critique of Pure Tolerance. Boston: Beacon.

WOLIN, S. S. (1960) Politics and Vision. Boston: Little, Brown.

––– (1968) "Paradigms and political theories," in P. King and C. B. Parekh (eds.) Politics and Experience: Essays Presented to Michael Oakeshott. Cambridge: Cambridge Univ. Press.

––– (1969) "Political theory as a vocation," Amer. Pol. Sci. Rev. 63 (December): 1062-1082.

WOLLHEIM, R. (1962) "A paradox in the theory of democracy," pp. 71-87 in P. Laslett and W. G. Runciman (eds.) Philosophy, Politics, and Society. Second Series. Oxford: Blackwell.

YOLTON, J. W. (1969) John Locke: Problems and Perspectives. Cambridge: Cambridge Univ. Press.

TERENCE BALL received his Ph.D. from the University of California, Berkeley, and is presently Assistant Professor of Political Science at the University of Minnesota. His articles, reviews and translations have appeared in a number of professional journals, including Philosophy of the Social Sciences, The Western Political Quarterly, The Review of Politics, *and* The Philosophical Forum.

A Better Way of Getting New Information

Research, survey and policy studies that say what needs to be said—no more, no less.

The Sage Papers Program

Five regularly-issued original paperback series that bring, at an unusually low cost, the timely writings and findings of the international scholarly community. Since the material is updated on a continuing basis, each series rapidly becomes a unique repository of vital information.

Authoritative, and frequently seminal, works that NEED to be available

- To scholars and practitioners
- In university and institutional libraries
- In departmental collections
- For classroom adoption

Sage Professional Papers

COMPARATIVE POLITICS SERIES
INTERNATIONAL STUDIES SERIES
ADMINISTRATIVE AND POLICY STUDIES SERIES
AMERICAN POLITICS SERIES

Sage Policy Papers

THE WASHINGTON PAPERS

SAGE PUBLICATIONS
The Publishers of Professional Social Science
Beverly Hills • London

Sage Professional Papers in

Comparative Politics

Editors: **Harry Eckstein,** *Princeton University,* **Ted Robert Gurr,** *Northwestern University,* and **Aristide R. Zolberg,** *University of Chicago.*